writing out the
STORM

To my daughter,

Jennifer Page,

who holds my heart,

and Shannon,

who never knew

that he gave me permission

to write, but he did.

With much love.

writing out the
STORM

Jessica Page Morrell

STARBOUND PUBLISHING
PORTLAND, OREGON

For a free catalog write to:
Starbound Publishing
P. O. Box 230986
Portland, OR 97281

Cover Design: Principia Graphica
Interior Design: Desktop Miracles, Inc.
Editor: Ann Granning Bennett
Author's Photo: Ray Bidegain

Distributed in the U.S. and Canada by
ACCESS Publishers Network

2 4 6 8 1 3 5 7 9

Library of Congress Catalog-in-Publication Data

Morrell, Jessica Page, 1953-
Writing out the storm / Jessica Page Morrell.
    p.   cm.
  ISBN 1-888054-26-3
    1. Diaries—Authorship.   2. Creative writing.   I. Title.
PN4390.M67   1998
808'.042—dc21

98–29891
CIP

"So from the age of twenty-four to thirty-six hardly a day passed when I didn't stroll myself across a recollection of my grandparents' northern Illinois grass, hoping to contact the older person I became to remind him of his past, his life, his people, his joys, and his drenching sorrows.

It became a game that I took to with immense gusto: to see how much I could remember about dandelions themselves, or picking wild grapes with my father and brother, rediscovering the mosquito-breeding ground rain barrel by the side bay window, or searching out the smell of the gold-fuzzed bees that hung around our back porch grape arbor. Bees do have a smell, you know, and if they don't they should, for their feet are dusted with spices from a million flowers. . . .

So, I turned myself into the boy running to bring a dipper of clear rainwater out of that barrel by the side of the house. And, of course, the more water you dip out the more flows in. The flow has never ceased. Once I learned to keep going back and back again to those times, I had plenty of memories and sense impressions to play with, not work with, no, play with. Dandelion Wine is nothing if it is not the boy-hid-in-the-man playing in the fields of the Lord on the green grass of other Augusts in the midst of starting to grow up, grow old, and sense darkness waiting under the trees to seed the blood."

RAY BRADBURY
Zen In the Art Of Writing

Contents

Introduction

Writing can take you to the deepest parts of yourself and along roads of discovery that you never dared imagine. Writing is also is a wonderful occupation, but in all honesty, it's scary as hell. I suspect that all writers are afraid. Of sitting in a room, alone, with a cold-eyed computer screen blinking an accusation, "What are *you* doing, here?" Then there are the maddening times when you're wrestling with a poem or story, and you can't describe a thing, and it's flat and vapid and stupid. You swear you're going to lose your mind before you get it right and decide that you must be crazy to write at all. Crazy because you spend hours struggling to find perfect words to fit perfect places, while you fight off your doubts and grapple with your need to be flawless.

So you sit down to write and find that you're scared. Of starting, of trying, of putting your bruised heart on the line and words on a page. But I believe that we can quell this fear, put it beside us like a sleeping dog, and write despite our fears, our doubts, our cowardliness.

You might be wondering, if writing is such a pain, why bother? The answer is easy: because writing is good for us. It deepens us, strengthens us, teaches us how be honest and patient and loving. Writing is both a practical skill and a way of connecting to ourselves and a bigger source. Becoming a writer will unleash our creativity, and in turn, creativity brings meaning to our lives. It all adds up to something wonderful.

The sad and strange truth of our times is that most of us are hungry, searching for more. This elusive "more" takes many forms—love, money, recognition, creativity, time with our children. A whole lot of us are exhausted, not to mention frazzled to the bone, trying to keep up with a race-the-clock schedule. There's a lot of searching going on in our culture and people are grasping at all sorts of solutions, from the simplicity movement to Buddhism to the old, reliable 12-step programs.

Writing is another path, a solution to needing more. I've been teaching writing and creativity classes for years, and I've watched my students apply writing to their simplest or noblest desires and seen the transformation that follows. I've heard hundreds of students read a piece of their history or some precious invention for the first time in front of the class. Many students begin by apologizing, explaining that what they're about to read isn't good, that they're new to writing, that they haven't had enough time to work out the kinks. Sometimes I think if I could collect all these apologies, they'd be tall enough to topple a skyscraper. The class is forced to sit patiently, squirming through their stumbling confessions, and then the room becomes still and church-like and words start spilling into the air. There's a sort of collective sigh that follows when they finish reading and something subtle shifts inside all of us. I wasn't raised Catholic but I imagine that the absolution that follows these readings is a little like going to confession. Good for the soul. Cleansing. Revealing. I've noticed that even if we hate the student's writing, we like that he or she had the courage to write it anyway.

Writing makes your life better because you get to speak your truth and turn a discriminating eye at this weird planet and tell other people just how you see things. Most people who write regularly, who make writing a crucial component in their existence, like themselves better than when they're not writing. It's really pretty simple. I know it works because it worked for me. If you write regularly—no matter what the subject or format—you'll shift your muddled worries to clarity, your vague hopes to reality, and your denial to crystal truth.

I've met the gamut of beginning and aspiring writers: senior citizens who are writing their memoirs, poets, journalists, would-be novelists, lawyers, young mothers, technical writers, people who keep journals, yuppies who want to sharpen their business skills. No matter what your reason for writing, if you keep at it long enough, you'll discover it has a kind of alchemical power. The more we write, the more we grow.

The majority of my students are between forty and sixty, and about ninety percent of them confess writing is a long-held desire. Sadly, they relate how they used to write when they were kids, teenagers, college students, but family obligations and jobs have gotten in the way. Now they don't want to prolong their dream. In my classes I've seen ugly ducklings transform into confident masters. After they shape their longings into essays and stories, they testify, mystified, that they never knew they had it in them. That is was too easy, too much fun. Or they whisper that their ideas came from a dream or a story their grandmother once told them.

My students and I have learned that once we write through the noise of our doubts, we reach a place of quiet. And that quiet within is both a respite and a marvel. Because the quiet is a lovely place of repose, but, then again, it's fermenting with words and inspiration. Before we get there, it's like we're hacking away at jungle overgrowth with a machete; but once we have carved a skinny path, we reach a sweet paradise of easy words and visions that blossom like gaudy tropical flowers.

I teach writing classes because I get to preach my version of the gospel: ***Persevere No Matter What***. I ought to know because I'm a born-again writer, a recovered wannabe. So, while lecturing about active verbs and metaphors, I sneak in Truth, which students usually don't want to hear. WRITING IS NOT FOR WIMPS. Or for dabblers, dilettantes, or the type of person who's only capable of half-assed efforts. Or for those afraid of the truth, of themselves, of the ghosts from their past. Writers can't be afraid of poverty or ostracism or what their mother thinks—we have to be made of stronger stuff. But how do we get out of bed each day, calling ourselves writers and settling ourselves into that sacred spot where words come forth? Instead of putting off our dream, we write anyway. We write no matter what's going on in our lives. We write, ignoring our cowardly heart rattling loud enough to shake our bones. We write despite distractions and agonies. We write when our family or the ghost of Mrs. Schultz, our third-grade teacher, looms at our shoulder and whispers that we're no damn good.

Then we write some more. Then we set some goals and eventually stuff our precious words into an envelope and mail it to a cold-hearted stranger. And return home from the post office and do it all over again. Until we die. Because writing feels so good when it flows, when you're on a roll. And it brings meaning into our lives. Really. Because once we conquer our fears, writing is about the best legal fun there is. It's right up there with sex and dancing, standing high on a mountain, or playing with little children who belong to someone else.

But first comes knowing ourselves a little better.

I'm forty-five years old as I write this introduction. This is the fifth version of this chapter, and each version moves closer to the truth, closer to who I am. I want to tell you what I've learned; why I and so many others have spent many years being wannabe writers before we found our way. Somewhere in this book is your life, too. It doesn't matter if you grew up in a city or my town of ten thousand. Or if your childhood was a *Father Knows Best* family of gags and laughing cousins and adoring parents, while mine was more complicated. We all have deep reasons, hidden reasons, unknowable reasons for why we don't write.

So, you must return to your past and find the kid you once were who likely had his or her head buried in a book amid the spinning world. Because writers are formed by the place they were born and the books they read. And writers were the kind of kids who noticed things: the colors of dawn, the heady smell of lilacs, the curve of their baby brother's elbow, shadows spread across the lawn like giants when the sun fell. You are all these memories. Because you were always a writer.

The small town I grew up in lives clear in my memory, filtering through my writing like a summer breeze lifting a lace curtain. Today I live worlds from that small town, but the truth of my life remains; I'm not like everybody else because I'm a writer. And I almost wasn't a writer because my early years scorched my confidence and flattened my heart. But along the way, I transformed my girlish longings and memories into stories. And then I made peace with my past, though some days it feels like a shaky truce between two Middle East countries who are both secretly hoarding biological warfare. And some days, many days actually, my childhood feels like a jeweled gift. I'm left with this jumble of sweet and sad memories, knowing I was always a writer.

What I've learned is that writers, no matter what their pasts, are by nature different from ordinary people because we notice everything and we travel inward to find a way outside ourselves. The wonderful news here is that we don't have far to go, only a few steps to our computers or notebooks. Maybe this makes us weird. Maybe this makes us outsiders, note-takers. Observers. Suspicious, since we hunker down with a notebook and create instead of selling plumbing or developing software for accountants. We've got dreams to weave tall as mountains, tales to spin galaxies wide.

Some of us write for the sheer joy of putting words on paper, but for others there are leftover hurts or a deep, dwelling loneliness begging to be healed. Most writers know that pain is eased by the company of words. So we write.

I began writing when I was a girl; poems, songs, stories. Like most writers I've had a lifelong love affair with books, preferring them to everyday life. Until I was fourteen, I lived in a small town in northern Wisconsin. I was the second-born, the oldest girl, and I've never looked backwards through a gooey veil of nostalgia; instead, I sifted through memories and learned to cherish all the good parts. This was probably the most worthwhile thing I've ever done because now I've reclaimed the magical pieces of my childhood. It was like washing a window grimy with years of grease and dirt and letting light into a lovely, treasure-filled room. In my remembering is a sweetness— simple rituals—my mother baking bread on Saturday morning, clover-scented summers and magical winter mornings, waking in the frozen dawn to find the feathery drawings of Jack Frost decorating the windows, the world muffled and buried in drifts of snow and white. A childhood spent mostly outdoors.

If as writers we're allotted a jigsaw puzzle of pieces to draw from, my puzzle box was full of material that a writer could use for years. The dark outline: the misfit girl, resentfully scrubbing the kitchen floor or peeling potatoes, while the rest of the family watches *Gilligan's Island*, the girl who was never told that she was pretty or that her poems were wonderful. The girl who turned to chocolate for solace, who told lies to get attention.

The good stuff: four seasons that were cherished and celebrated, fried chicken and mashed potatoes on Sunday, a pretty, clean house, and a family that appreciated all kinds of music—the strains of Tchaikovsky or Ray Charles filtering through the house, and a back door that opened to adventure. Writing about my past taught me that childhood is sometimes a strange dichotomy of the beloved and bitter, existing side-by-side like Beauty and the Beast. And my Beauty is a land not part of America anymore, a small town wrapped in rivers and trees and meadows. When I was a kid, a small town was a great place to be.

Our town held just enough. It was a poor town, the heyday of logging ended in the upper Midwest, but it was a pretty place, with rivers and tree-filled parks. My childhood held simple pleasures: the skating rink, the vine-covered public library, Devil's Creek, and the Wisconsin River and our tree-filled yard.

A life without frills, however, was a fertile start for a writer. We played games with few props, our tents were worn-out blankets pushed into the ground with clothespins, we made our own paper dolls, we fashioned our doll clothes from scraps of cloth. Each autumn we raked the fallen leaves into giant piles for jumping in, played hopscotch and jump rope, school, and red-light-green-light-hope-to-see-a-ghost-tonight. And I still hear our singsong voices calling through the dusk descending on a summer evening and smell the sweet scents of August.

My past has never left me. And through all the enchanted rhythms of the seasons I find reasons to write.

Like many would-be writers, life exacted its usual toll of pain and pitfalls, and I was sometimes blown off course. But there came a time when I decided to make writing my priority, and I finally settled in front of my computer and produced a steady stream of words. I began teaching writing classes and became an editor and taught more writing classes. The more I taught, the more I learned about writing and the more involved I became in my own work. I discovered that when I surrendered to it and put myself in the same chair, at the same time, day after day, my creativity entered like an invited guest. A lot of the time I wasn't all that thrilled with my progress, but then on some days the work was simply magical.

Along the way, I've shared most of what I've learned with my students. I've taught thousands of them now, and most have heard my growing-up stories, because within each of us lie rich tales and mysteries waiting to be told, our pasts a never-ending source for our work. I tell my students to write every day, to start small, to take their writing seriously, to *believe without a shred of doubt that they're endlessly creative.* In my classes, we strive to understand the *craft* of writing, putting perfect words in perfect places as Jonathan Swift said, snaring readers into a seamless reality. And it's just about the best fun we've had since we were kids.

Looking back, I can see the barrenness in my writing life only reflected the agony of an empty heart. I see the patterns of being stuck and blocked and just plain afraid to push myself until I got the words right. I see the early influences that shaped both my fears and successes. Sometimes it's like looking back on a long illness. Fear was the symptom, and the fear is finally gone. It's been a long road to this easy flow of words, this exhilaration that I experience as the words march across my screen.

I am convinced that you can find it, too.

The writing life lies beyond fear.

Write Anyway

"I don't believe for a moment that creativity is a neurotic symptom. On the contrary, the neurotic who succeeds as an artist has had to overcome a tremendous handicap. He creates in spite of his neurosis, not because of it."

ALDOUS HUXLEY

For years I searched for a magic elixir or a bridge that would carry me to the fabled land of writers. I imagined that I'd be miraculously whisked to this enchanting place, and, once I arrived, the mystical ability to write effortlessly would be bestowed on me.

I was sure that there had to be a miracle cure, an easy way. I bought all sorts of books about writing but usually didn't bother to read them. I researched markets for articles but didn't send any work to editors. Believe it or not, I wanted it bad. To be a writer. But not bad enough to devote my life to it. To organize my life around my dream of writing. I didn't pay my dues, and I didn't write consistently.

In other words, I was a wannabe. Fear kept me tiptoeing around the edges of the writing life for years. From time to time, I'd send out an article and get something published. Then I wouldn't try again for months. I'd talk about the books I was going to write but didn't attempt them. In my mid-thirties, I wrote and published regularly for a few years, but then, as I wallowed through a divorce, I drifted away from my free-lance career and took a job in public relations that was more secretarial than creative. Like many of my students, I allowed a crisis to sweep my dream away.

Call it painful circumstances or bad luck. Call it writer's block. I've had lots of experience with all of the above. Or simply name the REAL cause: FEAR.

Gradually, painfully, I learned the only truth that is worth knowing: the only way to be a writer is to write. The only way to be an artist is to make the time to create. And all my life, I'd stopped myself from writing because I was afraid of each step in the process, from first draft to marketing. I finally started facing my fears when I was in my late thirties.

I learned the necessity of writing regularly; writing when you are sad, tired, feeling nauseous, or hormonal. I learned the only way to learn the craft is to sit down and dance your fingers over a keyboard. Do it every day if you can. Write when it rains, write after your grandmother's funeral or the birth of your baby, when your car needs expensive repairs, or your cat just died. Write when your partner dumps you, your kid goes off to college, and your tomatoes have blight. Write as the rain forest is destroyed, the stock market dives, and your candidate loses the election.

Don't wait for the perfect mood or opportunity to write because it just might not come along. Forget about waiting for long, uninterrupted hours to start your great opus. Write when you can. Quit longing for a patron, a sugar daddy, or a free ride; instead find fifteen minutes, and sit down and write. There are few born writers; most of us have to hack away, learning as we go. Few of us feel worthy of the task. But we do it anyway.

Unfortunately, modern life is a sped-up, demanding existence. We're busy with the basics, just keeping food in the refrigerator and wearing clean underwear. When our schedules fill up, it's easy to put writing aside. But here lies the trap because before we know it, days pass, then months, then years, without making a consistent, organized, willful effort to produce regular writing.

I met a student recently who's changing careers because of health problems—a bad back. A lot of my students slouch into my classes and declare that they are suffering from job burn-out and are looking for a new direction. The student with the bad back is typical. He's in his forties and has always wanted to write but has never bothered to try. I questioned him about why he doesn't write. He says that all his years in school have made him afraid to start. Squelched. He never understood all those weird sentence diagrams and grammar lessons that decorated the blackboards of his grade school. He thinks that this confusion, going back thirty years, has translated into a general fear of writing.

Then he went on to list more fears. There were quite a few. Then he started naming excuses; he doesn't own a computer, his back hurts, he's great at research but not at translating his facts into sentences, he's afraid to market his work. . . . I listened while he rattled off all the reasons he doesn't write, then hit him with the only way out of his dilemma: ***WRITE ANYWAY.***

And, finally, that's all there is. ***WRITE ANYWAY.*** It doesn't matter if you're emotionally scarred because, when you were eight, Sister Mary Madeline smacked you with a ruler and screamed that you were an idiot. It doesn't matter if your neck hurts from an old whiplash injury or your teenage daughter despises you. It doesn't matter if you've never had a break, if you're low on will power. We all have hurts. We all have doubts, even nightmares. Most of us deserve more than we have.

Face your fear, find the will, name your dream.

You buy books about writing because you want to write. Somewhere within you, writing makes your soul sing. It's important. You have today, this moment, to start writing.

try this

Slip back in time and write about the first time you did something. Write about the first time you rode a bicycle, made love, hosted a dinner party, fell in love, fell out of love, traveled in an airplane, stood up for yourself, attended a funeral, told a big lie.

Beyond Fear

"Security is mostly a superstition. It does not exist in nature, nor do the children of man as a whole experience it. Avoiding danger is no safer in the long run than outright exposure. Life is either a daring adventure, or nothing. To keep our faces toward change and behave like free spirits in the presence of fate is strength undefeatable."

HELEN KELLER

There are dozens of fears that stop our writing. Fear stops us before we start, silences our beautiful voices before they're heard, kills our dreams before they're realized.

The blank page holds terror for all of us. Famous authors, prolific authors, still face with dread that first page, yawning and empty. Will the words come? Will they get it right? Writers have it hard. Sculptors have marble and clay, artists have paints, canvas, tools for their work. Writers have only our hearts, a desire to be heard and some tricks we've learned along the way. But it's enough. Despite our fear, we write anyway.

What are you afraid of? Are your fears rational or are they childhood ghosts still hanging around sabotaging your efforts? Creativity requires understanding yourself, giving yourself permission to take risks, then taking action. Start the process by naming your fears as the first step to confronting them.

Here are some common fears that writers might get caught up in:

I'm not very creative.
I'm not good enough.
Nobody will like my style.
Nobody will understand what I am saying.
I will be lonely.
My family will hate me if I write the truth.
What's the point? Writing won't make me happy.

My teachers were right. I'm lousy at this.

I'm not smart enough.

I'm not disciplined enough.

I don't know how to market my work.

The publishing industry is cutthroat; it's impossible to break in.

I'm not motivated enough.

I can't face rejection.

Writers are weirdos, alcoholics, losers.

You get the idea. The list can go on forever, but there is little substance to any of it. So let's throw some sanity, some reality in here.

Everyone is creative once we tap into the endless source within us.

You are enough. You are good enough.

If you stick with it and learn how to get the words right, someone besides your spouse will understand what you've got to say.

Motivation and discipline come from establishing a regular and nourishing writing routine.

The more you write, the clearer your writing becomes.

Your family will come around. Eventually.

Or it won't matter.

Loneliness passes.

The industry needs writers.

Writing is one of the best joys.

Rejection is only part of the game; it says nothing about the quality of your writing.

Writers are healthy and whole and wonderful.

I wish I could sell you the magic writing potion that I searched for all those years because I'd get rich and retire to Tuscany. From my Italian villa, I'd supervise my vineyard workers and gardeners while juggling calls from my accountant, broker, and business manager. All the while thanking the fates that created wimpy writers and made me rich. The potion, bottled in shimmering emerald glass, would taste like ancient honey mead. One sip and all our writing fears would vanish. Like a magical Prozac for writers. But *whoops!* this is the real world, and it's gray and raining in Portland, the dusky Tuscan hills are far away, and no such product exists.

Yet we *can* learn how not to be afraid. We weren't born afraid, we learned it. We began life as sunny little beings intent on exploring the whole world even if it meant tumbling down flights of stairs, falling off our bicycles, or risking our parents' wrath. Somewhere along the way, we got scared.

After we begin standing tall in our grown-up bodies and naming our fears, it dawns on us like a thump on the head in the dark, that being afraid not only stands in the way of our writing, but also our happiness, our self-regard. Once we tackle our fears, we start understanding deeper truths, and then our destiny beckons.

A common fear among writers is that deep down, we're not *really* creative. We read F. Scott Fitzgerald, William Faulkner, Ernest Hemingway, our literary heroes, and start whimpering and whining that *they're* the real talents. You finish reading a bestseller, then sigh piteously—after all, this is simply more proof that you just can't measure up. That you're second rate, not the real thing. What's the use, you moan? You'll never be as good as Stephen King or John Updike, Rita Mae Dove, or Charles Kurault. They're brilliant, and you're pitiful in comparison.

We assume that *other* writers were born under a benevolent sign, that they inherited a rich connection to a creative source, while we, unfortunately, don't have the keys to the kingdom. Clueless. Bereft, we chafe at our lousy luck. After all, it's all the luck of the draw, isn't it?

These assumptions are lies. They're also dangerous, limiting, and ridiculous. We are *all* endlessly creative. We all own rights to the same source. Creativity doesn't run in families like red hair or green eyes. It doesn't matter if no one in your family has gone to college, if you grew up on a truck farm in Georgia or in a ghetto in Philadelphia. *Creativity is your birthright.*

Creativity lives in all of us, unconnected to other parts of our lives. Believing in yourself, making your art a priority, then establishing a sustaining routine is what matters; everything else is just life. It doesn't matter if you are a vegetarian or a Big Mac addict, if you got straight A's in college, love nature or hate the outdoors, if you were raised as a Catholic or Methodist or Baptist, if you have money or can barely pay your rent, if you're twenty one or sixty seven, if you are single, married, divorced, fat, thin, short, or tall.

We are all creative and can learn to become more so by going deeper, by writing. For those of you who want to write, the source is there, but you must be willing to tap into it.

Read this again: *We are all creative. Creativity is our birthright.* Like the color of our skin, the curve of our brow, the shape of our nose. If your big fear is that you aren't creative, that only John Lennon and Sylvia Plath and Shakespeare were the real thing while you're a pathetic impostor, dump that belief. It just ain't so.

Fear is merely a bad habit.

And, like an addiction, fear is dangerous, insidious. It becomes an excuse, squelching our artistic attempts. Fear keeps us from putting ourselves on the line. But no matter how large fear looms over us, we must realize that fear is really cowardice. And that being afraid to write never justifies not trying.

Now is the time to admit that fear is not your only enemy, cowardliness is, as well. Soldiers are sweating with fear before they storm into combat, women are torn with dread when they're being wheeled into the hospital to face labor and childbirth. But the soldier still jumps from the plane and lands behind enemy lines, even though he's quaking so hard he can barely stand, and the woman pushes the wriggling baby into the world, although the pain is so wrenching and terrible that she's certain it will tear her apart.

Fear is a learned behavior that we can move beyond. Fear is an easy way out. Writing past the fear, that is, writing anyway even though we're afraid, isn't a short cut or a quick fix. But it's the only way. Writing past the fear is writing regularly, day after day, no matter what our mood or checkbook balance, until we finally realize that our creativity will always answer.

Writing beyond fear is writing until the words flow just right. Editing and rewriting, again and again. Sending out manuscripts. Believing in yourself when the world ignores your efforts. That's the hard stuff. Fear is too easy. It's the coward's excuse. It's not possible to be both a coward and a writer. Ask yourself what you're afraid of. Is this a realistic, grown-up fear? Be honest with yourself. How big is this fear? Does it need to be examined? Or is it an excuse to not try? To give up before you start? Write about it.

try this

Lie on your back with your eyes closed, your feet planted on the ground with your knees up. Take a few deep breaths. Relax and become still, just following your breath for a few minutes. Then let your thoughts drift to the reasons why you don't write. Let the first thoughts that pop into your head simply appear on the little screen in your mind, but don't judge them. What do you see? Now, look a little closer, still not judging or labeling yourself. Do these fears belong to a grown-up or a child? Now, say out loud, "I'm scared." Notice what new thoughts arise. What do you feel in your body? A tightening in your throat? A flutter in your abdomen? Where does the fear live in the body?

Take some more deep breaths. Say it again: "I'm scared." Pay attention to the thoughts, the pictures and images that filter through your mind, the twinges in your body. Keep saying the words out loud, noticing your reactions. Are you remembering experiences from your childhood? Go into the memory, relive it. Understand that these memories may be painful, yet may hold the key to your fears about writing. Keep taking steady, deep breaths, maintaining an awareness of where the fear resides in your body.

After you have experienced your fear, say out loud, "I feel the fear, but I'm going to write anyway." Repeat this saying, until you feel more relaxed. Pay attention to how this affirmation affects the anxious sensations you've been experiencing. Relax, following your breathing and letting your body be loose and comfortable. When you are ready, get up and write about your fear. Name it. Explore it. Fear is overcome by experiencing it directly in the body, then talking back to it.

Stuck?

If there is no wind, row.

LATIN PROVERB

We all know people who are stuck. Maybe your best friend has been in a bad relationship for years but never tries to fix it. Maybe your sister smokes, even though she's always talking about quitting. Or losing fifty pounds. Maybe you have friends who drink too much, spend too much, hate their job, are rageaholics, need to be needed. It's probably clear to everyone around them that they're miserable. However, when we offer suggestions—a 12-step program, a regular health-club routine, a therapist—they come up with all sorts of reasons for why they can't change.

I can remember that horrible paralysis. When I was younger, facing my fears was like stepping off a mile-high cliff. And once I ventured to the cliff's edge, there was no joy or comfort, only a hideous descent into a huge, dark emptiness. My fears controlled me for years, kept me in painful situations that I'd outgrown. But once I began creeping to the edge, facing my fears, changing my circumstances, I realized how powerful fear's hold was.

I also made an important discovery: that fear is a paper dictator. Once I confronted whatever I was afraid of—divorce, speaking the truth, moving to a new place—the fear toppled quickly. And best of all, I learned that as I took steps to change my behaviors, my sense of self changed dramatically. I still haven't achieved all my dreams, but I accomplish my goals one by one. And most important, I've recovered parts of myself that were overshadowed by fear; self-reliance, peace of mind, freedom, laughter. I'll never let fear paralyze me again.

When I teach fiction classes, I illustrate plot structure by comparing it to a mythic or heroic quest. I usually use Dorothy's journey in the *Wizard of Oz* to diagram my point. In most fiction, the plot involves a hero or heroine answering a call to arms that forces them to venture into a dark forest (their fears), face a terrible conflict, conquer whatever stands in the way along with their inner demons before they can leave the forest. Dorothy's journey through Oz illustrates my point. On her journey she faces the dark night of the soul, that forlorn moment when it seems that all is lost and she'll never survive. In Oz this moment comes when Dorothy is locked away in the hideous gloom of the witch's castle. Longing for home, terrified and certain that she's doomed, the cruel minutes tick away in the haunting, relentless hourglass. We've all seen the movie and know that the climax comes when she flings water at the witch and destroys her, freeing her slaves.

Once Dorothy and her friends survive this abyss and conquer the enemy and fears that were magnified in the dark forest, they are forever transformed, confident, and brave. And Dorothy, the Cowardly Lion, Tin Woodsman, and Scarecrow discover that they possessed the keys to their freedom and strength all along.

If you haven't realized that many classic and contemporary plots are built around mythic themes, look again at your favorite books and movies. What's the point, you're asking.

Facing our fears transforms us.

Becoming a writer is a heroic quest.

When we begin to write, we don't know if we're up to snuff, but we answer the call anyway. When we finally reach the forest we discover that it's tricky just getting around. It's dark, the paths aren't well-marked when it rains, it's impossible to keep our campfire going. When we get lost and try to orient ourselves, we discover that our Scout survival tips don't work, that moss grows on *all* sides of the trees.

Once we start writing, we discover that the path to getting published is strictly uphill, rutted, rocky, maybe slithering with snakes. The writing will come in uneven bursts at times. A dragon will appear. We'll lose our way. Some days we'll want to call it quits. Some days toiling at our computers will seem as grueling as tracking monsters through a bog. The forest, gloomy and eerie, moans and creaks with spooky, unknown noises. But ultimately, despite the pitfalls, we notice that the trees are magnificent, the air is pure and pine-scented, birds sing with a wild sweetness, and once through, we walk tall and proud.

try this

An easy way to move past our fear of writing is by choosing topics that are familiar and intimate. Since we all must eat—and most of us love to eat—write about food. Recall a fabulous Thanksgiving feast, the first time you tried to bake bread, a cooking class, your grandmother's molasses cookies or apple pie, and the treats and pleasures from your childhood. Write about oysters, sushi, chocolate chip cookies, Jell-O, guacamole, banana cream pie, hot dogs, wild mushrooms, and pasta. Write about hunger, chocolate cravings, vegetarians, dieting, obsessions, comfort food, and will power.

The Writer's Notebook

"For any writer who wants to keep a journal, be alive to everything, not just to what you're feeling, but also to your pets, to flowers, to what you're reading."

MAY SARTON

If only I still owned all the songs, stories, poems, and plots that leapt into my mind over the years. The truth is, I've lost a lot of my inspirations. Why would I be so careless, you ask? Because when I was younger, I didn't carry a writer's notebook and so neglected to stop and jot down my ideas as soon as they came to me.

We've heard stories about writers like Truman Capote who interviewed two death-row inmates in a Kansas prison, then returned to his hotel room to record, from memory, the text for *In Cold Blood*. Capote possessed rare memory prowess. Most of us must write everything down. The sooner we record our thoughts and inspirations as they pop into our heads, the better because it's likely that we'll forget most of them. Not only is there a danger of forgetting our ideas altogether, but these first inspired bursts are the most powerful. They have force, magic. We must capture our original thoughts like we're trapping an elusive, wild creature.

Buy a notebook that is portable, not too big, not too small. Carry it with you all the time. Now, look around with wonder, paying attention to everything. Eavesdrop on life. Write down every intrigue that comes your way. Use it as a sketch pad, a journal, a source. Find a format that suits, but get used to jotting in your notebook every time something strikes you. Make your writer's notebook so integral to your life that you feel naked without it.

This isn't a diary, however. Diaries are based mostly on our inner lives. Diaries are for our secret thoughts, our pains and grievances and struggles. Diaries, of course, are helpful tools for tracking tricky emotions, peering into the darkness, and noting our joys and successes.

Notebooks or journals, on the other hand, hold our inner thoughts but are focused primarily on the outer world where much of our inspiration lives. We use our notebooks to explore memories and notice common beauties and grace moments. Gradually we begin noticing that everyday life is touched with poetry.

You don't have to wait for inspiration to strike; just look out your window and notice it's everywhere.

Take your notebook to your favorite chair, slip on a jazz CD if you like, and start by staring out the window. Start with now. Notice the fly buzzing against the pane, the faded brick of the house across the street, the naked, yearning branches of the chestnut trees on the corner. Write about weather, autumn leaves, the deep November sky, your neighbor's Toyota, the first spring crocus.

Maybe from there you'll start spinning off, writing about springtime when you were a kid, how you'd search for pussy willows, robins, and dandelions for assurance that winter's bleak company was leaving town. Write about your first love, your sister, your secret dreams, your fears in the night.

Write about the dead cat sprawled beside the road, the mysterious Brillo pad that you spotted gleaming copper in the parking lot, the bottle of merlot that you shared with your lover and how its plum and berry flavors still linger in your memory a year later even though your lover is gone.

Carry your notebook in your backpack and write about hiking in a desert canyon, an alpine field brilliant with purple lupine, a night sky on a mountain spangling overhead like a million diamond necklaces, and how the shooting stars seemed to stop your heart for just a moment. Write about how you fall in love with the wrong people but have found lifelong friends. Write about your longing for a baby, your mother's funeral, your best friend's divorce, how daffodils in spring make you feel wild and young. Write about the curse of being beautiful. Write about the curse of being ugly. Write about growing old and how this is so surprising and sad and wonderful. Write about being ignored, bored, slurred.

Write about your tenth summer, when your best friend Margaret Bernstein had her leg in a cast and how you spent long hours with her playing Monopoly and Parcheesi instead of swimming and riding your bike. Recall all the details of those long-ago summer afternoons, the sun slanting onto the Bernstein's porch, Margaret's cast scratched with autographs, her naked toes incongruous and silly peeking from the plaster.

Take your notebook to a coffee house and write about your pregnancy and your hot flashes. Write about family secrets: your uncle's pornography collection, your Aunt Millie's mastectomy, your father's rages and brother's depression. Write about your landlord, your ex-spouse, your next-door neighbor, your granddaughter, your no-good son-in-law, the yapping Chihuahua down the block that you long to silence—permanently.

Write about the times you wandered through an art museum, dizzy with appreciation. Write about your favorite Matisse or Picasso portraits that hang in the Los Angeles County Museum, the Rembrandt, Degas, Cézanne paintings that you've lingered in front of, loath to leave their beauty. Write about the exhibit of Chihuly glass that found you walking dazed among the giant sculptures, drunk on color. Carry your notebook with you and sit under a fine old tree and write about all the artists whose sweeping lines and palettes and swirls make you almost weep with their power. Write about the intoxicating scents of an orange grove in April, movies that make you laugh or cry, thunder and lightening in May, and the thunder and lightening of forbidden love.

Take your notebook to a park and write about what your therapist thinks about your family, what your family thinks about your therapist and the homeless guy sleeping under the willow. Observe the children and mothers at the playground, and remember your daughter when she was six, and drink in the sounds of all the laughter rocking through the park.

Anchor your memories, chart your path, find your way.

But keep in mind that these notebooks are more than places to store our musings. These reflections become the SOURCE for our work. We record dreams, overheard conversations, strangers that frighten us, and news from the car radio. We remember childhood joys and outline plans for a difficult chapter. We recall the sensations of sitting under a dentist's cruel drill and the delicious thrill of a first, longed-for kiss.

Where does all this collecting get us? Our notebooks become a point on a map, a place to start, a way to hone our writing skills. And most importantly, notebook writing helps us push past our fear because we write only for ourselves. There is no pressure to be perfect or to show it to anyone, yet we notice our writing improving as our pages fill with words. And best of all, because we write when enthusiasm reigns, our notebooks become a source for longer projects. If we return to our notebook for inspiration, the perfect idea or phrase leaps out at us, and we'll be off writing like a greyhound bolting from the starting gate.

try this

Prowl office supply stores, discount stores or stationary stores, and search out your perfect writer's notebook. It should have a heavy cover in a fabulous color, be a convenient size, and contain pages that invite your words. After you buy it, immediately start carrying it with you everywhere, making notes to yourself as you go through your day. What does your world look like? Did you notice anyone unusual wandering past? Hear a great joke? A line you need to steal?

Take Yourself Seriously

"A few times on the journey . . . it seemed the abundance of sensory stimulation around us might make us expire. I wanted no more sounds or sights, no more flavors or fragrances . . . I stared at single words as clues. Sometimes notebooks are our calm companions, but other times they serve as crucial sounding boards, balance beams, rudders, oars."

NAOMI SHIBAB NYE

You'll succeed with your writing *only* if you take yourself seriously. First of all, take yourself seriously by creating a place to write, a space that is all your own. Call it your office or your sacred space. If you have to clear the dirty breakfast dishes off the kitchen table every time you want to write, this will be another obstacle to your intentions. You need an inviolable space for writing that is yours.

If you don't have much money to devise a writing place, improvise. For years I used a desk made from an old door perched on two file cabinets. It provided plenty of room for files, books, and my computer. Find a folding screen at a rummage sale, and cordon off a corner of the bedroom. A card table will do in a pinch, a ledge in the laundry room will suffice, a stack of orange crates and boards in a closet can be enough. Make a place that is your own. It doesn't have to be beautiful; it just has to be yours.

Now buy a bulletin board or devise a method where you can hang important papers at eye level. On your bulletin board list your immediate writing goals, one-year goals, and five-year goals. However, don't list forty-seven separate projects that you have to finish before you die. Don't decide you'll only settle for a guest appearance on *Oprah!* to prove you're a success.

Start small. Your bulletin board should inspire you to move on with your projects, not overwhelm or intimidate you. Make this list a workable plan. Choose three projects

to work on in the coming year, then prioritize them. Give yourself deadlines for these projects and decide how you'll measure your goals.

Now, thumbtack on your board a few photos of famous people or writers whom you admire who have succeeded against the odds. Pepper the board with inspirational sayings. I like, "Great works are performed not by strength but by perseverance."

Next, start collecting reference books. You will need a good dictionary and a thesaurus. A tool that is even better than a thesaurus is J.I. Rodale's *The Synonym Finder*. If you write nonfiction, buy William Zinsser's *On Writing Well*. If you're an aspiring journalist, purchase a copy of the *Associated Press Stylebook*. If you want to write mysteries or children's books, buy books offering tips on those genres. Aspiring fiction writers should pick up a copy of *The Art & Craft of Novel Writing* by Oakley Hall.

You say this sounds expensive? Buy your books at second-hand stores and garage sales. Borrow them from the library until you can afford to buy them. Ask your family or friends to give you resource books for Christmas or your birthday. There is always a way, and the bottom line is that if you want to write, you're going to have to invest in equipment.

Speaking of equipment, if you don't have a computer or word processor, you will have to buy one. This is the information age, and those of you writing longhand or plunking out your stories on manual typewriters can never hope to compete against computers and on-line communications. No money? Search the classified ads for used equipment. Shop the sales. Buy on the installment plan. Lease. Borrow. Beg from your family, your spouse, your boss. Writers write; they don't whine about how they can't pull off purchasing the equipment.

Now, get involved in the writing world. Check out the resources in your community. Go to book signings, readings, lectures. Attend writing classes and workshops. Join a writers' critique group. If you can't find one, start one. Clip book reviews and read author's biographies. Hang out in bookstores and libraries. Subscribe to *Writer's Digest* and *The Writer*. Read *Editor and Publisher* and the Sunday *New York Times Book Review*.

Meet other writers. Question them about how they solve plot problems, what they do when they get stuck on a project. Or borrow their marketing techniques. In the lonely world of writing, it's good to have some kindred spirits to cheer you on and support your efforts.

Here is a warning, however: don't just talk about your writing, *do* the writing. I've seen many would-be writers busy themselves with the business of writing: taking classes, sending for writer's guidelines, reading books on technique. Three years later, they still haven't finished a story or article, but they are full of plans for some day. Some day is now. Don't let anything take the place of writing. Writing comes first; the rest—the office, books, the computer—are merely tools. Writing isn't learned by reading writing books or sitting passively in classes. Writing comes with effort.

try this

Experts claim that it takes twenty-one to forty days for a new habit to become an ingrained routine. Choose a small goal like writing for ten or fifteen minutes each morning or writing one page every day, and act on your goal for thirty days. A mere month could mean a new life.

Procrastination

"Truth has no special time of its own. Its hour is now . . . always."

ALBERT SCHWEITZER

Often fear turns into procrastination. Not only do we postpone writing, we postpone starting, because, if we procrastinate, we don't have to experience those nasty pangs of panic that settle into our guts when we begin a project. Many writer wannabes fear most the beginning steps of a project, the first words. This isn't big news to most of us, but don't allow your inability to find the perfect first words to become a barricade that you can't move past.

Steal past the barricade with a few words. Your first paragraph doesn't have to be perfect; it only has to be there. Give yourself permission to write junk for the first draft. Don't worry about being pathetic or sloppy or affected. The first draft is for capturing a piece of yourself on paper; perfecting it comes later.

All writers, beginners and veterans alike, fear the first blank page or screen. It yawns as enormous as the Grand Canyon with no free rides to the bottom. If you procrastinate because you're afraid to start, outwit yourself by establishing a regular schedule or routine. Or try tricking yourself into writing by giving yourself rewards. Promise yourself an expensive restaurant meal, new lingerie, a CD, a weekend at the coast, AFTER you started your project. AFTER you're far enough along with the words that there's no turning back.

Sometimes tentative, can't-get-started writers remind me of teenagers playing "air guitar." You've probably seen them or done it yourself. You blast some Eric Clapton or Jimi Hendrix, pantomiming along to the music. A harmless pastime, you protest. But did you ever notice that most of the folks who play air guitar never bothered taking lessons or learned how to do the real thing? The point is that, for writers, fantasizing holds real dangers. For some beginners, fantasizing about writing takes the place of work. It's adolescent behavior and just another way of procrastinating.

The dedicated musician picks up a REAL guitar and plays the first faltering notes of "Three Blind Mice" or "Twinkle, Twinkle, Little Star." It's a measly beginning, but it's a beginning and therefore important. After the first attempts comes learning chords, endless practice until eventually the guitarist plays *real* Clapton songs. Stop procrastinating because it takes more energy than writing, and get down your first words, the equivalent of "Three Blind Mice."

Our fantasies about the writing life will never equal reality. It's more tedium than glamour, more diligence than inspiration. Avoidance is a natural response to hard work, like Tom Sawyer conning his friends into painting Aunt Polly's fence. But avoidance only brings immediate relief, not lasting satisfaction. Procrastinating keeps us standing on the outside looking in at our work, our dreams. This is a difficult place. It is just a delaying tactic: imagining yourself writing, dreaming elaborate visions of success, but not doing the work. Once you begin, you enter a new world, a world that is less bewitching than your fantasies but ultimately more satisfying.

Writing brings us close to our self, our visions, our soul. Art lives within us. It must be entered. Have faith, go within, start writing.

try this

List topics you've been meaning to write about and add them to your writer's notebook. This list of writing topics is a back-up system, a nudge when you're feeling lazy, motivation when you're uninspired.

The Body's Wisdom

"Remarkably, material also is the writer's attempt to control his energies so he can work. He must be sufficiently excited to rouse himself to the task at hand, and not so excited he cannot sit down to it. He must have faith sufficient to impel and renew the work, yet not so much faith he fancies he is writing well when he is not.

"For writing a first draft requires from the writer a peculiar internal state which ordinary life does not induce. If you were a Zulu warrior banging on your shield with your spear for a couple of hours along with a hundred other Zulu warriors, you might be able to prepare yourself to write. If you were an Aztec maiden who knew months in advance that on a certain morning the priests were going to throw you into a hot volcano, and if you spent those months undergoing a series of purification rituals and drinking dubious liquids, you might, when the time came, be ready to write. But how, if your are neither Zulu warrior nor Aztec maiden, do you prepare yourself, all alone, to enter an extraordinary state on an ordinary morning?

"How to set yourself spinning? Where is an edge—a dangerous edge—and where is the trail to the edge and strength to climb it?"

Annie Dillard

Writer's block, the temporary silencing of creativity, can happen to anyone. I believe there are two causes of writer's block: fear and the body's wisdom.

Wisdom and writer's block share the same source: the inner self. We all have many layers of consciousness, including the wise, deep part of us that is tuned to our personal rhythms and inclinations. There are many names for this inner wisdom, but, for the purpose of this book, we'll refer to it as intuition. As humans we're aware of the cycles of nature; seasons, lunar phases, eclipses. Yet we often ignore our own inner seasons, our intuition. The Bible tells us that "to everything there is a season, and a time to every purpose under heaven." Eastern religions like Buddhism recommend living a contemplative, mindful existence, achieving a deep awareness of the inner person and inner rhythms.

Writer's block that is caused by fear can be overcome; silence that comes from an inner cycle must be acknowledged, then moved through. How is this accomplished? First, by slowing down and becoming quiet. Quit fretting, worrying, cursing yourself, anguishing. Surrender.

Next, become still and listen to the messages your intuition is sending. It's saying it doesn't want to write. It wants a pause, a rest, a realignment.

I have discovered in my own struggles with writer's block that it occurs when writing no longer makes me happy. I have friends who also write for a living, and we all write because we love it. Writing is part of us. It's hard work, but it's also play, pleasure, joy. Writer's block looms when writing becomes a chore, an obligation, a job. And I've turned into a bad boss; bullying, single-minded, shoving myself into chains, dragging myself to the computer.

Creativity responds to pleasure, not bullying.

Visit a preschool class of four year olds. This time of year, November, the walls are decorated with construction paper turkeys of improbable, delicious design. The turkeys are fat, orange, brown, cross-eyed, wobble-legged, silly, wonderful. The cluttered bulletin boards display an amazing array of finger-paint drawings. The colors exist in the brightest, richest hues: yellow, pink, blue, green. Notice the spontaneous, raw, creative energy amid those wild swirls. Take a long look at the other art projects that decorate the room: pilgrims, autumn leaves, art made from macaroni, cotton balls, buttons, string, smears of color, all jumbled together with joyous abandon. The message is clear; creativity is fun. Creativity is childlike, unfettered, free. Look around the classroom again. No blocked artists in sight, right? When kids are handed paper and paints, they dive right in, creating art without agonizing and without doubts.

Give yourself permission to have fun with your writing. Or take a break from it. Read. Go for a walk. Visit an art gallery, a museum, a forest. Try another format. Write a poem, a limerick, a soap opera, a letter, a comedy routine. Try painting or assembling a collage, cook a huge pot of stew or paella. A word of caution here: I'm not advocating surrender or suggesting that you give up writing. I'm advising that you realign yourself. Sometimes it's necessary to step back to rediscover the joy in our work.

Try remembering times when you were happily immersed in a creative project. How did it turn out? How old were you? How did your body feel while you were creating?

Silly? Giddy? Like time stood still? Write just for fun for a while. Sometimes as writers we must abandon our work ethic and dip into our childlike parts in order to write freely.

try this

Borrow a beginning. Finish a story after borrowing one of these first lines as a starting point:

When you wake up in jail, you know it's going to be a long day.

Felicia was the kind of woman who caused men to _____

My family has always pretended that _____

In the middle of the night, when you're wide awake and miserable with wanting to sleep, _____ is what you think about.

All my life, I swore that I'd never stoop to _____. Then I met Andrew.

Like Yourself

"The mind is the writer's landscape, as a mountain scene might be the landscape of a visual artist. Just as a visual artist studies light, perspective, color, space, we write out of memory, imagination, thought, words. This is why it is good to know and study the mind, so we may become confident in its use and come to trust ourselves."

NATALIE GOLDBERG

Tragically, many of us emerge from childhood with a shaky sense of self. Some twenty-one-year-olds are lucky; they're confident and lovely creatures, bright-eyed toward the future. Those of us who enter our twenties or thirties burdened with doubts instead of buoyed by confidence must learn how to like ourselves no matter what our childhoods were like.

Loving or liking yourself is another ingredient in the writer's repertoire. People who like themselves persist in the face of obstacles but, most importantly, possess a deeper source to write from.

As I've said, writing comes from a deep place in our consciousness, where past and present merge. Words and inspiration issue from layers of consciousness that we'll never fully understand: buried memories, unconscious needs, moods, dreams, intuition.

As writers, we plunge into these depths like a diver risking the bottomless ocean. Along the way you'll meet darkness, mystery, swarms of fish, coral reefs, caves, danger. As writers we *must* look within, dive deep. The inner world holds our words and inspirations. Writers need to uncover memories, find the eight-year-old who collapsed in a giggling heap at the silliest jokes, who flew homemade kites into the gusty March wind, who first fell in love with storytelling while reading *Gulliver's Travels*. This childhood is a wonderland where our creative sparks ignite.

For some of us, delving into our past is painful. Hellish. We've heard theories about self-esteem but doubt that it applies to us. After all, what does this have to do with writing? Working with students, I have witnessed hundreds of reasons why they don't write even though the desire is there. And from what I've seen, there are infinite sources of pain and conflict within blocked writers. I'm not a therapist, but I have a few suggestions that might shed some light.

First, we all need to understand that self-esteem is linked with our ability to forgive. This is my personal nemesis because I can hold a grudge long and hard. My definition of forgiveness isn't a pious, born-again concept. Forgiveness merely means that we have finally let go of another person's influence over us so that he or she has no power to hurt us. Maybe you haven't forgiven yourself, your brother who always got your parent's praise and the best presents, your cousin the molester, or your parents. True, they were not perfect; in fact, maybe these people were truly despicable and maybe their behavior towards you was unfair or monstrous.

What we're talking about is detachment, how you *react* to these people, how much energy your interactions steal from your precious hoard. The past is a place to visit, to understand ourselves and deepen our writing; but the hurts from another era can't be the gatekeepers to our words.

Write a letter to whomever wronged you, venting, spewing your guts, and then don't send it. Or write a letter *from* your tormentor to you, and in those pages have them apologize and assure you that you're wonderful. Or try affirmations, prayer, chanting, meditation. Find a therapist, a self-help book, a support group, whatever it takes. If your head is cluttered with old grudges and resentments, clean up this toxic sludge and move on. Recently I heard a psychologist explain that most of us will never understand the roots of all our behaviors. However, we can shine our awareness on our behaviors and then apply will to make the changes that need to happen.

If this talk of forgiveness and psychology is making you nervous, relax. And have faith.

Writers are influenced by all events, traumas, and triumphs that came before the moment we're living in now. Trauma or "unfinished business," as it's called, blocks our way, becomes another barricade to writing, prevents our gilded words from getting to the page.

Or maybe your self-image is out of date, that is, you see yourself as you were fifteen years ago when you were a lumpy, slouching, unhappy teenager, not as the dynamic and capable person you've become. Maybe the teenage you was too afraid to write, but the adult version is dying to write a screenplay or a collection of poems.

Think about it; if every time you dive inward, you meet sharks and inky darkness, writing will be a struggle. If deep down, you really don't like yourself, you'll probably have a hard time writing. I can't cite a famous scientific study to prove this statement. Judging from my own experience and observing lots of writers, however, I've come to believe that emotional health and unlimited creativity are somehow linked.

I've noticed that my angriest students have the most trouble writing. And I've also noticed that my writer friends who are balanced and consciously live in the present get the most writing done. When I look back to my earliest bouts with writer's block, I know that it matched my low self-regard. I didn't like myself much when I was younger, and writing was torture. I was too bitter, too angry, too sad. The more I like and respect myself, the easier the words come. Unfortunately, I can't teach you specifically how to find your way, only suggest that you try.

Like everybody else, I have bad days when all I want to do is weep and wallow in profound self-pity. Sometimes I catch myself gossiping, and I hate myself. Some days I'm lazy or manic, obsessed or depressed. But I know as surely as summer follows the pale green buds of spring, people can grow and bloom and my latest bout of insanity will pass. That I will get back on track. That ultimately, I am healthy. And that self-regard and a peaceful heart are basic ingredients to any writer's art.

And finally, writers must learn to be kind to themselves. One of my friends made an important discovery. She purposefully tuned into her inner chatter and started paying attention to what she was saying to herself. After listening to the vicious litany of self-criticism and abuse she heaped on herself, she realized that she wouldn't dream of treating other people as badly as she treated herself. Eventually, she was able to quiet her inner critic and begin the difficult but rewarding task of being gentle with herself.

Revel in your strengths and talents. Listen to your friends when they compliment you. Talk to yourself in gentle, soothing tones, as if you were a kindly parent kneeling to comfort a frightened child.

try this

Tape reminders and affirmations on your bulletin board, on the bathroom mirror, next your bed. Write "I LIKE MYSELF" and hang the words in front of your writing desk and repeat it one hundred or one thousand times a day if necessary, until you beat back the beast of self-doubt.

Put Writing First

"I will tell you what I have learned myself. For me, a long five or six mile walk helps. I have done this for many years. It is at these times I seem to get re-charged. . . . But if when I walk I look at the sky or the lake or the tiny, infinitesimally delicate, bare, young trees, or wherever I want to look, and my neck and jaw are loose and I feel happy and say to myself with my imagination, 'I am free,' and 'There is nothing to hurry about,' I find then that thoughts begin to come to me in their quiet way."

BRENDA UELAND

———————————————

Life is complicated and busy. On good days we manage to wear clean, ironed clothes and socks without holes. We race from work to the delicatessen to the dry cleaners to home. Once home, we help our kids with their homework, throw in a load of laundry, squeeze in some PTA phone calls and the work we brought home from the office. Around eleven we collapse exhausted into our beds, an hour later than we'd planned. Weekends are filled with errands and unclogging drains and trips to the hardware store and the kids' soccer games. We schedule rare get-togethers with our friends in our daily planners. There is barely time to call our mother once a week, how the heck are we going to cram writing time into all this bustle?

The answer to finding time for writing is simple: PUT IT FIRST. Make it your first priority, then allow the rest of your schedule to fall into place. Once you commit yourself to this simple concept, life gets easier.

When I was younger, I let days, months, and years slip by without writing regularly. And the truth about all those wasted hours when I didn't write was that on some level I was miserable. I didn't respect myself. I didn't have faith in myself because I wasn't doing what my heart called me to do. Because I wasn't putting writing first.

The only way to achieve our writing goals is to establish a sustaining routine to shore us up against the ebb and flow of life. This schedule, of course, will be determined by your day job and family obligations. If you don't already own one, buy a daily planner or a giant desk calendar. Block out the time obligations that are non-negotiable: work, church, chauffeuring the kids to and from school, walking the dog, meals, classes. The hours that remain will seem pitiful, too few to fulfill all your dreams.

Now schedule a block of writing time into each day. In my classes, stay-at-home moms despair over their crowded schedules, endless obligations, and interruptions. Putting your writing first takes ingenuity. Maybe on Mondays and Wednesdays you can only squeeze in twenty minutes of writing before breakfast, but on Tuesday your neighbor watches your kids, so you can snatch four luxurious hours for writing. Block the four hours in your daily planner with a bold, red pen and faithfully adhere to your plan. No matter what. Even if the house is a mess, there's a mountain of laundry and a dozen errands to run and phone calls to make. Even if it's the first day of spring. Even if you aren't happy with how the writing is going. Even if your mother is in the hospital. Visit her *after* your writing time. It is a sacred commitment to your future. It is fundamental to making it as a writer, instead of wallowing forever with that gaggle of lazy wannabes.

After the kids leave for the morning, turn on the computer and while it's booting up, throw a load of towels in the washing machine and sit down to write. When you need to get up for a stretch or bathroom break, toss the towels in the dryer, but don't linger in the laundry room; head back to the computer, and write some more. When your four hours are up, gather your kids at the neighbors, take them out to lunch, and run a few errands on the way home. Read your little darlings a few stories, then settle them in for their naps. While they're sleeping, clean the kitchen, start another load of wash, and make phone calls. By the time the children wake, the day will be almost over, and it will be time to worry about dinner. But it was a good day, because you got your writing in. If you started your morning chatting on the phone (complaining to your best friend about how you don't have enough time to write) or grocery shopping or mopping the kitchen floor, chances are you wouldn't get around to your writing at all. Put writing first; a little dust won't kill your family, but dust gathering on your dreams is another matter.

Schedule your writing time before you schedule your favorite TV programs, exercise routine, phone calls, movies, or cocktail dates. Schedule the writing first, and, I repeat, stick to the schedule. Let's say that again: Schedule the writing first and then fit in your hobbies and "down time" after you write. Put it first no matter what. If your plan says that you're going to write every day from 4 to 8 a.m. until your novel is finished, then set your alarm for 3:50. Many first novels have been written in the early hours of dawn. Is it easy? Heck no. At least not at first. But once you've established a schedule, it becomes a routine, then a habit. And sooner than you think, you'll start looking forward to your routine.

Remember when you were in grade school and your teacher rewarded that "A" on your book report with a gold star on a big chart that hung in the front of the classroom? Remember how proud you were when Mrs. Wallace planted stars next to your name? You were recognized, rewarded, and it felt good.

Borrow one of those kid-like motivation techniques. Hang up a calendar that you can use to mark your progress. On every day that you write your quota, give yourself a check mark, an "X," a star, a goofy sticker. Or record the number of pages you finish each day. Hang this calendar where you will see it every day. Too silly? Then invent another system, but keep some kind of visual record of how many hours you spend writing every week. You're probably not going to like keeping track of yourself at first. Most adults believe this is penalizing and demeaning. Maybe it reminds them of all the things they hated about grade school. Annie Dillard said that the way you spend your days is how you spend your life. You have to keep track of yourself.

Tracking yourself isn't a punishment, it's about training your awareness. This is like telling food addicts to keep a diary noting everything they shove in their mouths. At first they balk at the task of recording their calories. Then, once they get used to admitting to every potato chip and brownie, they're amazed at how often they eat, because so much addictive eating is done in a blind, unaware haze. Similarly, a writer's day is occupied with a hundred tasks and obligations, and we plod through the precious hours blindly, not noticing that there are a dozen opportunities each day to slip in our writing.

Maybe you've fooled yourself into believing that you spend hours writing each week, when actually those hours are riddled with daydreams, interruptions, doodling, doing the dishes, chatting on the phone, everything but accomplishment. When you establish a visible reminder of your daily output, you'll notice immediately when you slide into a rut and start letting days slip by without writing those precious words. Your progress calendar will make you accountable, and it's best if it looms accusingly in front of your desk.

One last bit of advice about establishing a routine: while you're planning your days, set aside some time each day to quiet your mind, gather your energies, become centered. In 1938 Brenda Ueland wrote *If You Want to Write*, a brilliant little book. She crams a world of advice into her chapters and is one of the first professionals to recommend that writers take time out each day to go for long, rambling walks so that their minds can wander free. I believe in walking early in the morning and find that some of my best writing ideas swim into my awareness while I'm wandering around my neighborhood noticing flowers and trees. I'm lousy at meditating, but one of the most prolific writers I know meditates twice a day. Other writers in my circle practice yoga, tai-chi and African dance. I know many writers who spend quiet time gardening in order to refresh their source of words. So when you're planning a routine, add some time, about twenty minutes or half an hour each day, to still your mind.

Most of us feel fabulous, drained, and exhilarated when we finish a project. Nothing is a bigger kick than typing "the end" on the last page of a manuscript. It's a taste of heaven. And it means you've got bragging rights. So tell the world when you've finished a difficult chapter, mailed out a manuscript, sold an article, filled a notebook. Then bask in the compliments.

Consider giving yourself more tangible rewards. Maybe every fifty pages of final copy could win you a new writing book, hot fudge sundae, massage, new dress, or basketball tickets. Your rewards should represent luxury. Adhering to a writing routine deserves acknowledgment.

try this

Write the words, "*Nulla dies sine linea,*" near your work space. It means (in Latin) "never a day without a line." Next, block out your writing schedule in your daily planner or calendar. Be realistic and set small, doable goals. How about thirty minutes or one page a day for starters? Tell your family about your goals and post your writing schedule for everyone to see. Try to write at the same time every day because your unconscious mind will respond to your new routine and assist your creativity.

Start Small

"Now I want to tell some things I have learned about writing from my class.

"Though everybody is talented and original, often it does not break through for a long time. People are too scared, too self-conscious, too proud, too shy. They have been taught too many things about construction, plot, unity, mass and coherence. . . .

"Another trouble with writers in the first twenty years, is an anxiety to be effective, to impress people. They write pretentiously. It is so hard to do this. That was my trouble."

BRENDA UELAND

———————————

Beginning writers must take themselves seriously, carve time and a space to write, but then should consider slowing down. Don't take on the grandeur of becoming a *WRITER;* instead, realize that writing is a lifelong apprenticeship. A *WRITER* has grand allusions, expectations. *WRITERS* expect to slip to the top of the best-seller list without breaking a sweat. But expectations interfere with writing. Reframe your thinking; consider writing a lifelong task, a practical, hands-on learning process. Write because you must because writing makes the sun rise in your heart.

Start small. Big projects are intimidating. Big projects can silence you. Write in your notebook, try your hand at a scene, a poem, a song, or maybe a blueprint for a larger project. If you've always dreamed of writing a novel but have no experience with the format, you're probably dooming yourself to failure by attempting a novel as your first project. Practice. Write descriptions, character biographies, settings. Describe a beach, a cardinal eating sunflower seeds from a feeder, an empty theater, a castle, a hospital room, or a space ship. Write about an old couple holding hands as they stroll through the mall, little girls having a tea party, crows fighting over garbage, boys arguing in the street.

Your early projects needn't be grandiose; they only need to be finished. A dusty collection of unfinished novels or epic poems is a deadly reminder that our writing or willpower isn't up to snuff. When you start small, you have a chance to achieve small goals that eventually lead to larger ones. Practice, practice, then practice some more.

try this

Snatch small bits of time and write a paragraph, a stanza, a brief description. Most of us won't have long, uninterrupted hours for our writing, but we can slip in fifteen minutes during our lunch hour or when we first wake up. Scrutinize your days for modest openings to further your goals. Take your kids to the library and sneak in fifteen minutes of research. While dinner simmers on the stove, make informational phone calls. Scribble a letter while the baby naps and plan your letter to the editor while you commute to work.

Silence Your Inner Critic

"The way I treat my writing is the way I treat myself. It was one of those profound understandings. It's as if my writing and my psyche are one. That the writing is the deepest part of myself. When I ignore it, I'm just not paying attention. Then I'm living a conventional life, and living it by rote, but I'm not attending what we call self in that deep way."

DEENA METZGER

Childhood is a lot like being in the army. Kids are surrounded by a host of drill sergeants types, who, with their best interests in mind, boss them around and make them toe the line. Adults are trying to keep kids safe, teach them responsibility and discipline. However, sometimes their methods fall short of a Mr. Rogers' neighborhood approach. Usually without being aware of the damage done, adults in authority keep kids in line with criticisms, rebukes, and threats. Or maybe the adults were gentle and well-meaning, but their constant nagging to be careful and don't-poke-your-eyes-out admonitions got stuck in our heads, and we learned to be tentative.

Whatever your childhood was like, most us grow up with our minds cluttered and haunted by a litany of adult voices. The wounding words of childhood are hard to erase and years later still limit us. For writers, they are still another deadly barrier to the creative self. Here's how it goes. Let's call our typical writer wannabe Ron. Ron has always dreamed of writing fiction, but he puts it off until he turns forty-nine and wakes up the day after his birthday and tells himself that its now or never. Poor Ron, as the years slipped by, he just couldn't find a spare moment to write. It's time to buckle down, he tells himself. No more excuses. So he's heading toward fifty, his hairline is receding, and it's time to take control. Feeling both guilty and relieved, he finally settles at his desk. The computer screen flashes on, and he pauses, contemplating the opening scene.

Since Ron's been planning to write a novel for a long time, he has a great plot worked out. He's always been a Jack London fan, so he's writing about a guy living in a remote cabin in Alaska whose wife, Martha, leaves him in the middle of winter. Martha can't stand the cold, and the seclusion, and most of all, her husband's deadly silences. Once she leaves, he's faced with discovering himself, and this terrifies him. Ron starts by naming his character Alex. He decides to throw in some more conflict, a violent winter storm that piles up snow for days, encounters with hungry, slavering animals outside his door, a dwindling fuel supply. Great stuff, he assures himself. Plenty of conflict. He can almost sense the biting winter cold, as he imagines his character, Alex, alone in his cabin with the wind howling outside his door.

Funny thing is, though, Ron doesn't know *how* to start. He knows he has to paint a scene, where Martha finally abandons ship but can't decide what finally motivates her to drive off in their only four-wheel drive vehicle. He tries a few vague, half-hearted attempts, but the words just aren't coming. He decides to slip into the kitchen for a snack. While he's up, he decides to call his mother who hasn't been feeling too great lately. Twenty minutes later, after polishing off a roast beef sandwich and chatting with mom, Ron is back facing the empty screen, fighting panic, when it happens; a fusillade of critical messages start pouring into his head:

"You call yourself a writer?"
"Give it up. Your dad was right. You can't write and never will."
"Face it, you've got no talent."
"Who the hell do you think you are, Henry James?"
"Don't quit your day job, you jerk."
"Your ex-wife said you'd never amount to anything, and she was right."

The messages from his past, those criticisms and commands from authority figures meant to keep him in line, have turned into the Voice of Judgment. He's heard these bitter invocations before, and now he's listening in spite of himself, paralyzed with doubt.

Ron, like many of us, is responding to the inner critic, the Voice of Judgment, believing the messages as they race through his head.

The triggers that set off the harsh words of the inner critic can be anything. A blank page or empty computer screen, a rejection letter in the mail, spotting your college roommate's story in a national publication. The Voice of Judgment, like a chorus of ghosts, sends shivers down your spine and into your soul. As these cruel voices intrude, your confidence withers, and writing slows, sputters, stops. The inner critic robs your motivation, then your dignity.

There is another name for the inner critic, the Voice of Judgment: saboteur.

There is only one solution. Silence the inner critic, the saboteur.

Easier said than done, you whine.

Let's go back to our writer friend, Ron. The poor guy is stuck with those nasty voices beating him like a cruel master whipping a dog.

The way to silence the critic is to make a move. Ron needs to start writing. It doesn't matter if he can't write the first scene; what matters is that he can write something. Let's say he's fascinated with the weather in Alaska, because he's a native of northern Michigan and remembers the long, bleak winters of his youth. In fact, those crummy winters are why he lives in California. Instead of listening to the inner critic, he begins with his memories of Michigan winters. Ron starts writing about howling winter winds, snow swirling furiously, burying everything, six-foot icicles, deadly, sub-zero temperatures that freeze exposed skin in minutes.

Ron is feeling better now, writing about the storm. Suddenly, he has an inspiration; maybe it's a dim memory from his childhood, he's not sure. But he decides to add a dog to his plot, a stray that appears nearly frozen at Alex's door. Ron likes the idea of this dog; he can see that there's lots of dramatic potential with another character in his story. He writes the scene with the dog, and he's off and running. Eventually he'll write the beginning of the story, but the important thing is that he's bypassed the critic and involved himself in his creation.

I advise my students to free-write regularly, that is, to simply put down words without any concern for form, content, or grammar. The main reason for free-writing is to bypass the inner critic. We need to write fast and furiously, not caring about anything except getting some words down on the page. Writing anything, no matter what the content, allows us to sneak past the hawk-eyed critic.

I'll say it again: the inner critic is silenced by a steady stream of words. Write about catsup, eggplants, boredom, lampshades, your first car, your father's favorite chair, your sixth birthday, a letter to your future self. It doesn't matter what you write; it just matters that you write something that intrigues you and pushes you past the critic.

You say that it's impossible to silence your critic? You say that you need the critic's judgments because otherwise you might write junk?

Critical judgment is fine. It's what editing is all about.

We usually write first drafts that are lousy. This is *not* a problem; in fact, this is the way it should be. I'll repeat this concept because it's important. *Most, if not all, writers*

write lousy first drafts. Either we whip that pathetic first draft into shape with a serious rewrite, or we dump it and start over. There's no harm in listening to ourselves when a draft lacks polish. This is discernment, this is wisdom.

The inner critic, on the other hand, is the enemy. The difference between the two is the *tone* that the inner critic uses. It is harsh, accusatory, and, most important, it is rooted in fear. And fear has no place in a writer's repertoire. Fear's role in our lives is to challenge us but never, never stop us. Don't let the inner critic sabotage you. Instead, write heart-emptying garbage, poems to Allah, a fairy tale, silly openings. It doesn't matter. Your words just have to breathe; they don't have to be gorgeous. Ease past the critic, outwit this devil, tell him to shut up and leave you alone to write in *peace.*

try this

Start your day with a free-writing session. Free-writing means writing without worrying about spelling, punctuation, or grammar. It means scribbling down words as quickly as you can without worrying about meaning or content. Free-writing is a doorway that leads to a steady flow of words.

The rules are simple. Open a notebook. Start writing. Don't stop to think. Keep writing.

Notice Everything

"The first week of October in southern Vermont is the unbearably beautiful American time and place. Brilliant yellow birch-covered hills slope down to glowing green meadows. Every sugar maple along every country lane combusts in scarlet and gold. The autumn sun brightens the white church steeples in the pretty valley towns. Plump pumpkins appear in orange pyramids outside the crossroads stores, and the smell of wood smoke hangs in the air. The intensity of the season so overpowers the senses that autumn cannot be remembered from one year to the next, so its splendor always comes as a shock."

CHARLES KURALT

Has this ever happened to you? You're driving along, traveling your regular route to work or speeding down the freeway to your friend's house, when you "come to," that is, realize that you don't remember the last five or ten miles of your trip? You've zoned out, operated the car on automatic pilot.

Unfortunately, many us operate on automatic pilot much of the time. Some of this tuning out actually makes sense. Routine makes life easy. The ordinary, the common place, the predictable make it easier to cope with the mountain of details and obligations that swamp our days.

Then again, zoning out is a kind of self-protection. It's a noisy world out there. Advertisers are hawking at us constantly, music pours from car radios, sirens screech, airplanes roar overhead. Amidst all this noise and sensory input, we retreat, we shut down, or at least *long* to escape.

But writers can't retreat. Writers *must* notice everything. Writers must hone their senses to a keen awareness. Not only is the noise and color of life the stimulus for our work, but ultimately it enhances creativity. A creative mind is one that is exercised and lively and, most of all, observant.

We are drawn to babies and small children, not only because they are adorable and cuddly, but because of their fresh perspective, their unbiased, clean look at the world. A few months ago, I was walking a Dalmatian puppy, a favor for a friend. As puppies go, he was frisky and handsome and attracted admirers as we pranced past. I couldn't help but envy his fresh responses to the world around him. He noticed every leaf scattering on the wind, every cat, dog, squirrel, twig, and piece of garbage in his path. His ears strained at every car horn and dog barking, and he paused often to sniff appreciatively at the lively smells of the city neighborhood.

I have another memory, a party on the Fourth of July a few years back. Outside a small town in the high desert of eastern Washington, friends were throwing a Hawaiian-style pig roast. The night before, a pit was dug near the barn, and the pig was wrapped with giant tea and banana leaves flown in from Hawaii. The coals were ignited at midnight, and, in the early hours of morning, the pig was buried. The next afternoon, guests started arriving, mingling outdoors, as the rich smells from the roasting pig floated through the air.

I remember the host, bleary-eyed from his night-long task, wandering the outskirts of the party, greeting friends, but not making much sense. Children swirled through the yard like whippoorwills, and there was a huge ice-cooled tub of wine and mineral water.

Later a tractor with a small crane pulled the steaming, swinging, smoking pig from the pit and dumped it on a huge slab of plywood. I joined another guest to carve up the pig, and digging into the beast with my outsized knife felt as foreign as carving a buffalo. As I sliced the pink, steamy meat, the party goers swarmed the buffet table and filled their plates with pork, potato salad, tomatoes, and pasta.

But most of all, I remember the last moments of the party when I held a baby whose name was Guy. I was happy holding Guy, and part of the reason for this was that he reminded me of my daughter years ago. I stood in the road, amid the haunted stillness of nightfall with Guy warm in my arms.

Then the fireworks from the small town a few miles away began.

The first burst of red sparkles that spangled the dark sky caught Guy by surprise. He started, his little body jerking in amazement. With each colorful explosion, he cooed and gasped, his eyes wide and bright, his body squirming towards the sky. Colors and sights for which he had no words.

Does this mean that I'll write a story about a pig roast or a baby at a fireworks display? Maybe. But probably not. The larger point is that my memories are rich because of my acute observations. The party memories are woven with all the sights and sounds and smells. I could write more about the fragrant clumps of herbs in the garden or the dusty,

rolling landscape of the Horse Heaven Hills in the background of the farm. The point is, I took the time to record the details of that long day. Notice everything, then infuse your writing with the details.

try this

Use your writer's notebook to note the blemished, odd, and ugly stuff that simmers around you. Explore the undertow, the sadness, the pain in your world. Write about corruption, brutality, the dark side. Don't turn away. Write about the old lady down the block who carries her dog around, the disheveled woman who mutters to herself on the bus, the teenager next door who sports a dazzling array of tattoos and nose rings, the residents at your grandmother's nursing home, and the creep at the office who hits on all the women.

Notice The Ordinary

"Each man has his own way. After all, most writing is done away from the typewriter, away from the desk. I'd say it occurs in the quiet, silent moments, while you're walking or shaving or playing a game or whatever, or even talking to someone you're not vitally interested in. You're working, your mind is working, on this problem in the back of your head. So, when you get to the machine it's a mere matter of transfer.

"What is an artist? He's a man who has antennae, who knows how to hook up to the currents which are in the atmosphere, in the cosmos; he merely has the facility for hooking on, as it were."

HENRY MILLER

Notice the ordinary details of your neighborhood. By paying attention to the ordinary, we force a clarity into our writing. By noticing the ordinary, we paint more details into our writing, a comfort to the our readers. We enliven our writing with the specific sights and smells and sounds around us all the time but often overlooked. Writers can't afford to ignore the ordinary since it breathes life into our work. Noticing the ordinary sharpens our powers, enlivens our imaginations and senses.

Imagine that you paid your seven dollars to see a movie made by a trendy young director, and, as the last opening credits rolled past, you're shocked to discover that he's staged the whole film against a white backdrop instead of a set or location. Impossible you say, no one would buy a ticket for anything so empty. Anyone who's seen a blockbuster like *Jurassic Park* or *Titanic* knows that movie sets are painstakingly created to look like real life or the elaborate fantasies of the creators. The details pull us in, help us believe in the actors and the plot. Set designers orchestrate cars parked along the streets, building designs, shadows, fire hydrants, traffic lights. The ordinary.

What is the ordinary? Everything we pass by without really noticing. Start by paying attention to the common sights in your neighborhood: cats, fences, sidewalks, basketball nets, shrubs, mailboxes. Some spiritual disciplines advise us to stay in the present, to practice mindfulness. It's considered a way of life, a meditation, a Zen approach to daily living.

Notice houses with red doors, gold Volkswagens, white Accords, crows and sparrows. Notice how many fountains or bird baths you spot as you walk through your world, your neighborhood. How about window boxes? Have you seen any lately? Do you know the names of the flowers growing in them? Find out. Stretch. As you move through your days, how often do you see young girls with braided hair? Dogs wearing sweaters? Homeless people with shopping carts? Diaper delivery services? Cowboy boots? Red shoes? Couples arguing? Billboards? Men in bow ties?

And what about the background sounds? You should notice sounds, not block them. Savor all the noise in your environment, then insert sounds into your stories. The distant swish of cars on the freeway, birds chirping, squirrels scolding, wind rustling tree branches, a helicopter's chop-chop-chop, a motorcycle varooming past, children's laughter, a door slamming, an engine coughing, a saw whining, a lawn mower clattering, and bus brakes screeching. The ordinary world is magnificent. Pay attention.

try this

Write an essay, poem, or story that is based on an ordinary detail or a simple memory. I've written essays that were inspired by lilacs, soup, shoulder pads, and working out with a trainer. For examples of how the ordinary can be transformed into wonder, read the poems of W.S. Merwin.

The Eyes Of A Child

"Concentrate on what you want to say to yourself and your friends. Follow your inner moonlight; don't hide the madness. You say what you want to say when you don't care who's listening."

ALLEN GINSBERG

Remember my story about Guy's first fireworks? When the first brilliant colors exploded in the night sky, he was startled. But then, with each colorful explosion, he cooed and reached up towards the lights, enthralled. The great joy of parenthood is witnessing our children's "first times." Their first tottering steps, first encounter with a kitten, first bite of birthday cake or ice cream, first bath, first haircut, first ride on a merry-go-round; these are all precious moments.

The rush of emotions that parents feel is difficult to describe; these are prideful, lump-in-the-throat, misty-eye moments. I remember the first time my daughter pulled herself upright in her playpen. She stood, delighted with herself, triumphant and wobbly-legged, so proud of the new height. I still can see her baby grin.

The world for young children is filled with marvels, enchanted seasons, fresh delights. As a writer you must borrow their naiveté, see with the eyes of a child. Experience the world as if it were brand new. Look close without judging. Creativity research notes that a common trait among inventors and scientists is that they approach their work with childish wonder. This wonder is a crucial component to creativity. If a scientist can't step outside the normal and perceive a problem with a fresh perspective, the options are blocked, the vision narrow. Being open to new sights and ideas expands our problem-solving abilities.

Read biographies about artists, musicians, and inventors. Hang around children and notice how *they* notice the world. Try adopting a pure, unbiased scrutiny of your

surroundings with your old perceptions abandoned. Allow only wonder. This fresh perspective will enhance your writing, breathe life into your words.

try this

Sit in a place where you normally wouldn't hang out, and imagine that you just landed there from a distant galaxy. You have no vocabulary or context for any of the sights you see before you. Or imagine you have just undergone a miraculous surgery that restored your eyesight after years of blindness. What is out there? How can you experience it as brand new?

Pay attention to the shapes, shadows, and curves of the world. The way the wind tugs at leaves and branches and stray wisps of hair. Notice peoples' eyes and how they gesture with their hands, hold their bodies in a crowd. Watch wheels spin around as vehicles whir past. Count clouds, pigeons, sea gulls, cracks in the sidewalk. Read the graffiti on the subway walls, the religious tracts in the Laundromat, the advertisements on the sides of buses. Examine a flower or plant leaf, noticing the delicate striations of color, the mysterious stamen, the fragile veins.

Change Your Routine

"Seize the day. Trust tomorrow as little as possible, since envious time will have fled even as we talk."

HORACE

Shake yourself up by experimenting with a new routine. Try it on for at least three days. If you normally go to bed at ten and rise at seven, go to bed at eight and rise at five. Take the bus to work instead of driving your car. Or walk, ride your bicycle. If you must drive, travel a different route to your usual destinations each of the three days. While commuting, pay attention to your surroundings, search for pink flowers, women wearing hats, or green neon.

Change your writing routine. Write at 5 a.m., immediately after work, at midnight by candlelight. Write in bed, at the library, in a diner, at a shopping mall. Write sitting on the floor, in front of a roaring fire, at the kitchen table, on the front porch, in a tent, by a campfire, on a park bench, next to a duck pond.

If you always skip breakfast, try some hot cereal or a hearty breakfast of eggs and sausage. Do you usually brown bag it for lunch? Visit a restaurant. Or spend your lunch hour browsing in a bookstore. Eat your tuna sandwich next to a fountain or an outdoor sculpture, in front of a fabulous painting at an art museum. Write a poem, a plot outline, a dialogue scene during your coffee break.

Take a long walk at dawn, at dusk. Drive to another part of town and walk along a river, a beach, in a neighborhood quiet with grand mansions. Stroll in the rain, walk through masses of fallen leaves, through new snow. If you usually read classics, read a contemporary author. Grab a friend and go for a ride on a tandem bicycle. Hike in the woods. Rent a hansom cab and snuggle with your lover, pretending you live in another era as the horse clop-clops along. Do you spend evenings chatting on the phone with friends or watching television? Turn off the television, ignore the telephone. Write letters,

your memoir, read inspirational works, attend the symphony, the ballet, bake bread with a six year old.

There is a great risk in being only half alive; if day after day we adhere to the same routine, we will not have the keen awareness that fills our writing with delicious details.

try this

Extend yourself by writing stories that are told from someone else's point of view. This technique is especially helpful if you choose a narrator or main character who is at a dramatically different stage in life than you. Twelve is a strange, difficult age. We are caught between the worlds of childhood and adulthood, not yet a teenager but changing dramatically.

Write from a twelve year old's point of view:

A gang member in a large city.

Someone whose parent has just died.

Someone whose parents are getting divorced.

An immigrant arriving at Ellis Island.

A plains Native American before resettlement to a reservation.

The son or daughter of a Tibetan sherpa.

An Iowa farm kid.

A captive on a slave ship.

A member of a family crossing the country on the Oregon Trail.

A Jewish youngster preparing for bar/bat mitzvah.

A young Pakistani rug maker.

Been There, Done That, Got The T-Shirt

"'Who will teach me to write?' A reader wanted to know.

"The page, the page, that eternal blankness, the blankness of eternity which you cover slowly, affirming time's scrawl as a right and your daring as necessity; the page, which you cover woodenly, ruining it, but asserting your freedom and power to act, acknowledging that you ruin everything you touch but touching it nevertheless, because acting is better than being here in mere opacity; the page, which you cover slowly with the crabbed thread of your gut; the page in the purity of its possibilities; the page of your death, against which you pit such flawed excellences as you can muster with all your life's strength; that page will teach you to write.

"There is another way of saying this. Aim for the chopping block. If you aim for the wood, you will have nothing. Aim past the wood, aim through the wood; aim for the chopping block. . . ."

ANNIE DILLARD

Sometimes my most difficult students are the ones who claim that they've already done everything possible to succeed at writing and insist that the world is stacked against them. These types tend to be surly at best, with attitudes that run the gamut from pessimistic to hostile. They're often on a mission to discourage the whole class, determined to drag everybody down to their own private hell. Bitter, they can recite a litany of terrible wrongs done them. Angry, they often have an editor or someone to blame for their misfortune. Discouraged, they usually have a few manuscripts moldering and yellowing in a desk drawer. I suspect or have witnessed that they haul out these faded dreams only when they've been drinking.

While I've met lots of disenchanted writers, most of them fall into two categories. The first group is rather young—say twenty-three to thirty with a novel or two (usually science fiction) already under their belt. These young writers often send their books out to anyone even vaguely affiliated with the publishing world and are collecting a discouraging pile of rejections. When I gently suggest that maybe they should chalk up their first book as a learning experience and start a new project, they look at me like I'm suggesting they cut their toes off and string them together as a necklace.

The second type are usually fifty-something, and they too have a book or two written, but they don't bother to market it because, according to them, the publishing world is filled with vipers. While the young wet blankets are hollowed-eyed and haunted and alternately incensed that the world doesn't realize how brilliant they are, the older burnouts are furious because they're running out of time. When I delicately suggest that the older writers might benefit from a critique group, they assure me that they can't find anyone talented enough to show their work to.

These students display such an unappetizing array of traits that I hope that they'll hate me on sight and drop the class after the first meeting. They are rarely the best writers in the class, yet they often have cruel criticisms about the other students' work. They usually don't read widely, but spout know-it-all, scathing condemnations of the best authors around. The bitter types often choose obscure topics to write about, usually don't have a clear idea about who their audience is, and believe they don't have anything left to learn. They often don't know the meaning of word patience; they have a maniacal glint in their eyes and a rage that only psychotherapy can cure.

If any of this sounds familiar and you think I'm writing about you, it's time for a makeover. Swallow your pride, take more classes, and join a critique group. Ask for help and pay close attention when people give you advice. Get rid of that chip on your shoulder, and remember why you started writing in the first place. Because it's fun. Because writing makes you feel alive and vital and involved. Because you have something important to say. Stop fuming and start listening. Cut out the self-pity and try another approach. Find professional writers, and ask them how they broke in. Start over, re-invent yourself. Learn how to praise other writers and appreciate their techniques. Be grateful. Be kind. Get over yourself.

try this

Join a writer's critique group. If you can't find a writer's group in your area, start one. Ideally your group should have at least five or six members. Set up the ground rules at the first meeting. Decide when, where, and how often you'll meet. Decide how many pages you'll be bringing to each session and how you want to voice your opinions about each other's work. Remember that a critique should be tactful and balanced, including positive and negative feedback.

Persist

"Nothing, unless it is difficult, is worthwhile."

OVID

Persistence is probably the most overlooked virtue. Pulitzer prize writers aren't born, they're shaped from years of work. The coveted prize comes after a long apprenticeship, writing word after word after word.

Writers must persist in the same way as athletes persist, by practicing, over and over.

Have you ever visited an inner-city playground and watched the young men playing basketball? The players spend long hours, their rubber balls echoing again and again against the brick walls and asphalt school yards. Have you ever observed the lone hopeful, a child shooting endless free throws at the hoop long after the sun has dropped from the sky? In the inner city, there aren't many dreams. But there is Michael Jordon and Magic Johnson and heroes who, like them, were once boys on a playground, aiming at the backboard. Again and again.

In most communities there are driving ranges for golfers to practice their golf strokes and tennis courts where players hit balls against a practice wall, perfecting their serve. If we happen to stroll past and notice these athletes perfecting their techniques, we don't explode into laughter, mocking their foolish dreams, their devotion. No. We admire people who persist, who practice.

Dentists go to school to learn how to fill cavities, lawyers study years in law school, therapists take classes in psychology and social welfare. These professionals labor long hours over their books, amass debt, serve as interns, start as junior partners. When they graduate from college, they start at the bottom of the law firm or clinic, accumulating skills as they mature. In other words, most professions require that we pay some dues to succeed.

Yet, many writer wannabes don't understand that writing, like other professions, requires an apprenticeship. That, like everybody else, they've got to pay some dues. A lot of beginning writers fully expect to be promoted to CEO without starting out in the mail room. The fact is, writing requires a probation period, and it is usually unpaid. Wannabe writers believe they're going to become famous merely by declaring themselves like Athena born full grown from the head of Zeus. They imagine if they take a class or two and browse through a few writing books, that's all it takes to become a writer. They are wrong. We are all rookies, students, greenhorns, when we start. Michael Jordan didn't get to be Michael Jordon until, no matter where he was on the court, he could hit the hoop with a startling precision. Before that, he was just another kid with a dream. It took years.

So how do you persist? Start small so that you become accustomed to writing as part of your daily routine. Commit yourself to fifteen minutes of writing practice every day. Fifteen minutes is easy. It's the time you spend eating dinner or talking on the phone. Imagine that fifteen minutes as part of your daily hygiene routine; you shower, you brush your teeth, you practice writing. Write every day. Write when you don't feel like writing. Write when the words seem bland, meaningless, or scary. Keep learning, practicing, trying. Persist in the face of all your doubts and exhaustion. Persist.

try this

This concept is worth repeating: Early morning, when you are still bathed in the last dreams of dawn, when your consciousness is misty from sleep, is rich for writing. Start with the dream you were experiencing before you woke, then start writing quickly whatever comes to mind.

Some writers need a topic to jump-start their free-writing session. Write about the dewiness of dawn as you slip reluctantly from the dream world into morning. Write about: bananas, babies, Picasso, snails, root beer, hang gliding, bird songs, bunny slippers, apples, TV detectives, blue jeans, teenagers, soap operas, hot chocolate, wet dreams, acne, fairy tales, plumbers, dating disasters, intuition, nightmares, meditation, illness, war, silence, merry-go-rounds, diapers, snails, bubble baths, revenge, aquariums, road trips, zoos.

Free-write, first thing. You will feel accomplished and in control. Try it. Fifteen minutes, first thing.

Writers Dreaming

"I write because I want more than one life; I insist on the widest selection. It's greed plain and simple. When my characters join the circus, I'm joining the circus."

ANN TYLER

I awake late, that is, at 7:30, and quickly move to my computer to record my dreams. My dreams are epics, filled with improbable dramas, pain, mystery, celebrity appearances, and indecipherable puzzles. I often don't understand my dreams, but I always pay attention to them. Why? Because the enduring message from my dream life is that I am immeasurably creative. My dreams have recurring metaphors and images: food, babies, worries, and illness.

Today my dreams are typically strange. In the opening scene my sister and I are driving a golf cart in a festive parade of Disney characters marching into a large arena. The bleachers are lined with spectators, music plays, spotlights trip through the crowd.

Then my identity shifts, and I transform into one of the seven dwarfs moving through the crowd, my giant, oversized head perched above a woodsy-type costume. Treading along the edge of the rink. I feel the cold emanating from the ice.

My identity changes again, and I am now dressed as Snow White.

The dream shifts, and I am in my hometown in northern Wisconsin. I give directions to a woman on a bicycle, instructing her in how to find the church that I attended as a kid. I describe the mile she is going to travel, block by block.

The last dream of the morning takes place in a small restaurant. I am having lunch with a chef from Seattle. We're served by a strange waiter who makes jokes that we can't understand. I order a steak for lunch and drink a dark beer from a wine glass. In real life I haven't eaten a steak in more than twenty years. I mention this in my dream and notice that the steak doesn't have the usual texture, that it's rice-like. The chef is nervous, it's a long drive back to Seattle, and he has much work to do yet that day.

What is my point, you ask? Why bother to pay attention to all this detail, this confusing jumble of images and scenes?

Dreams are magical stories that illustrate how to frame life metaphorically. Dreams remind us of our natural storytelling abilities when we recall the rich details of our nightly visions. Dreams are the mother lode for writers, a mine so deep and grand and inexhaustible, you need explore only a portion of its vast wealth.

You are still not convinced. What's the big deal? In recording these dreams, I am giving you the bare outline of my dream experience. My dreams were alive with color and smells and a cast of hundreds. The second dream featured the massive, stained-glass windows of the church, where a gentle-faced Jesus holding a shepherd staff stood among a meadow of lilies. Sunshine lit the stained glass, illuminating the glass in golden hues and shimmering jewel colors. These images were full of texture and life and possibilities for me as a writer. It's not the actual images that interest me but rather the *seamless quality* and *wholeness* of the images.

The emotions in the Disney dream were strong; I wasn't good enough, out of my depth, confused, worried about my appearance. I can transplant the essence of these emotions into a character or explore how they affect me as a writer.

Dreams are rich, lush, vivid, confusing, mysterious—all these things. Their inspiration to writers is endless. They are movies we get to attend every night without paying a dime for admission. Dreams provide both amusement and startling insight. They assure us that we are all storytellers, myth makers.

For those of you who can't remember your dreams, take heart. Everyone dreams every night. If you can't remember your dreams now, search out ways to recover these precious visions. There are books and techniques available to learn how to remember, understand, and record your dreams. Find the books, learn the techniques, notice the amazing details of your dream life. Then allow your rich images to feed your writing.

try this

Re-read some of your entries from your morning free-writing sessions. Notice how you've recorded your dreams and their rich, mythical texture. Next, use a dream as the basis for a story, poem, or essay. For inspiration, watch a video of the Disney film *Fantasia.*.

Write About People

"The purpose of art is to produce something alive, in my case, in print, but with a separate, and of course one hopes, with an everlasting life of its own. The miracle is that it should live in the person who reads it. And if it is real and true it does, for five hundred years, for generation after generation."

HENRY GREEN

Most of us have been profoundly influenced by a teacher, coach, relative, or friend. Some of us met the most important people in our lives when we were children, others step in to guide us through our college years, or hang fast while we're going through a mid-life crisis. Maybe we met our best friend at the playground while our kids argued in the sandbox. Some of us meet our lifelong friends, mentors, and guides when we least expect it, at a party, a class, or meeting.

No matter where we met our special friends, we soon recognize their importance and influence. They serve to open a door, shine a light, model behaviors that we want to adopt as our own. Stop and consider what your life would be like without mentors. Take a moment and think about the wisdom that they taught, the laughter you shared, the understanding that you never questioned. Remember the first teacher who spotted your talents, the coach who recognized your natural abilities. Think back on their qualities that you've consciously or unconsciously tried to emulate. Maybe your family was quick-tempered and volatile, while at the Johnson's house, your next-door neighbors, you watched that family treat each other with kindness and gentleness. You vowed that when you grew up you were going to be a dad just like Mr. Johnson. Perhaps your guardian angel was a stranger who nursed you through your tonsillectomy or called 9-1-1 when you were mugged. Recall how they have loaned you strength and driven you to the hospital and accompanied you to the lawyer's office and took in your children when you couldn't cope.

I'll always remember that my crippled grandmother saw my potential and believed in me. And I wish that I could tell her in person that she was right. But grandma is long dead, so I write about her and other people who have helped me along the way. I write to express gratitude, hoping that my voice, somehow, is heard through the years.

try this

Write about a person who has influenced you. Was your grandfather your hero? Did the gentle words of your great-aunt Helen keep you sane during a hellish period when you were at odds with your parents? How about your teachers, childhood friends, and the neighborhood bully? How did these relationships shape you?

Write About Objects

"We're supposed to be able to get into other skins. We're supposed to be able to render experiences not our own and warrant times and places we haven't seen. That's one justification for art, isn't it—to distribute the suffering? Writing teachers invariably tell students, Write about what you know. That's, of course, what you have to do, but on the other hand, how do you know until you've written it? Writing is knowing."

E.L. DOCTOROW

———————————

Sometimes I assign students a list of unrelated objects and tell them to write a short story or piece based on these objects. The results are usually amazing. I don't have a profound justification for my assignment, except that it's fun and pushes my students to connect disparate ideas within a connected framework.

Yet there is a deeper lesson here. The small objects that surround us—our clothes, furniture, knickknacks, jewelry—shape our identities and tell our stories. Do you collect sea shells, coins, antiques, plants? Do you wear vintage clothing? Drive a '68 Falcon? What do your belongings mean to you? Have you tried describing them on the page or putting them in a story?

try this

Choose one of the lists below and spin a story, about five to seven hundred words based on the objects.

I.   Tangerine, Radio, Trout, Scissors, Pekinese, Soldier, Skyscraper
II. Siamese kitten, Bible, Geraniums, Colicky baby, Mountain top, Mashed potatoes, Staple gun
III. Singapore, Race track, Gorilla. Convent, Moon, Bestseller, Lawyer
IV. Snowstorm, Chocolate ice cream, Boom box, Monk, Willow tree, School bus, Hammer
V.   Lasagna, Black beaded purse, Born-again Christian, Bowl of prunes, Prize fighter/boxer, Convertible, Orphan

EXAMPLE: A story based on List V. of unrelated objects

WITNESS
Dorene Warner

" . . . truth, nothing but the truth, so help me God."

"State your name please."

"Sarah Elaine Webster." Her braces softened the s's.

"Miss Webster, you knew the deceased?"

"Yes, we were neighbors for five years, and we had been friends since college."

"And do you know the defendant?"

"Yes. Bart . . . Mr. Barton moved into the building three years ago. I first meet him in Caroline's apartment. She had baked him some **lasagna** to say 'welcome to the building,' and he came to return the dish. I went . . . a co-worker had given me a box of fruit from her garden, and I took **a bowl of prunes** over to Carol. That's when I met him."

"Do you have knowledge of their relationship?"

"Oh, yes, Caro and I talked about everything, or at least we used to. She told me he was a **born-again Christian** and an **orphan** . . . that he had no family, no one at all. I think that's what made him want to control her."

"Objection."

"Sustained."

"Miss Webster, what did you observe directly that made you think Mr. Barton wanted to control Miss Morrison."

"His car, to begin with. He drove a **convertible,** a classic, he said. She could ride in it, but he would never let her drive it."

"Was there anything else?"

"I could see the pattern, but Caro didn't see it, or didn't want to see it. He insisted that Caro be with him all the time, except when she was at work. After a few months he changed jobs and started working near her office so they could go to lunch together. And then he started driving her to and from work, to save her bus fare, he said. He was never more than five minutes away from her, twenty-four hours a day."

"Why did you think this behavior was anything more than devotion, a demonstration of the love the defendant felt for Miss Morrison?"

"Because he scared me."

"Miss Webster, why were you afraid of Mr. Barton?"

"He was into fitness . . . that bothered me. He worked out every day, weights and stuff, not at one of those spandex-and-music places, at a gym just two blocks from her office. Caroline said he'd been a **boxer or wrestler**. I asked her once if he was on steroids, but she said he wasn't."

"Why would you have asked your friend that question?"

"Because he beat her up, more than once."

"Objection!"

"Overruled."

"Please tell the Court why you believe Miss Morrison had been beaten by the defendant."

"She had 'accidents,' lots of accidents. There were black eyes, a sprained wrist, a dislocated shoulder once. She always made up some excuse. I saw bruises on her arms. I went over on the thirtieth of December, because I wanted to borrow her **black beaded purse** for New Year's Eve. She was wearing her bathrobe, and the sleeves fell back when she reached up into her closet. There were ugly bruises on her upper arms, both arms. I tried to ask her about it, but Bart came into the bedroom."

"Did Miss Morrison ever tell you those bruises and injuries were caused by the defendant."

"No, she didn't. But then, we never were alone to talk, he was always right there in the room. I was going to talk to her on the tenth . . . the tenth of January. We were invited to a baby shower for another friend, and I knew Bart wouldn't be able to go with her, and I had planned . . . I was going to ask her then. But she was killed the evening of the ninth."

"Do you have any other information about Miss Morrison's death?"

"Yes. When I told the detective about the bruises on her arms, he told me that they were still visible . . . when they performed the autopsy."

"No further questions."

Beyond Loneliness

I won't lie to you. The writing life is sometimes lonely. Being a writer requires spending long hours alone on your private mountain top. At best, the writing transports you to other worlds, far beyond your mundane concerns. Some days it's a little dull to have only your thoughts as companions during your writing sessions. At worst, the lonely hours at your computer can yawn as empty and bleak as Antarctica.

The only solution is to write through the loneliness.

Loneliness needn't be endured; instead, it can become transformed. Some days I approach my desk, and I am desolate, empty, self-pitying. I'm certain I'll never have enough love, money, or laughter. I'm convinced that I've made a huge mistake, that writing isn't worth all the sacrifices I make.

I carry my misery, doubts, and loneliness to my computer. I start writing, and inevitably something magical happens. After I've spent half an hour or so at my computer, I feel calmer, less alone, less unsure. More time goes by, and the little black words

march along the screen. This isn't so bad, I tell myself, I can do this. I keep writing; the radio in the background nags for my attention from time to time, but creativity is my real companion on these mornings. As the words fill the screen, my loneliness diminishes and finally disappears.

Sometimes I admit the words aren't enough, and I need stimulation, people, connection; so I take a break and walk through my neighborhood or run an errand. I can do this now because I know I'll come back to my work, my writing. In my younger years, if I walked away from the project, I might not be back for weeks.

Sometimes I make a phone call when I'm lonely. I've been cultivating a group of friends whom I can call during the day when I hit the loneliness wall. Or I write letters to friends who live in other states. If I need more inspiration, I read other writers' solutions to their creative problems. I surround myself with creative types. We call each other when we're stuck with our work, critique each other's manuscripts, and celebrate each other's successes. There are many solutions to the loneliness inherent in a writer's life, but the main answer lies in wrestling it to the ground, facing the monster by writing.

try this

Time travel to the future and invent your ideal life. Pretend that you've been writing regularly for five years and you've achieved your writing goals one by one. What are your mornings like? How do you spend your weekends? How have you designed a sustaining routine that keeps you on track, day after day? Who are your friends? Do you have a mentor? How many hours a day do you spend writing? Have you written a novel, screenplay, column? Do you have a publicist, agent, business manager? Visualize.

You Are Endlessly Creative

"It's because we associate creativity with the unique position in our culture. It's true that we can't all be Einsteins, we can't all be Beethovens, so if we think of creativity as that success and recognition, then it's true we can't do it. But each one of us can experience the feeling of discovery that these people had. We may not have the luck to occupy the niche of an Einstein, but we can certainly appreciate the mystery of the universe, the beauty or harmony of how nature is put together, like fantastic clockwork. All of these things we can learn about, we can participate in, we can enjoy, and at that level, that kind of creativity is what really makes life full and worth living."

MIHALY CSIKSZENTMIHALYI

Within each of us lives a magic genie, a kind of Aladdin figure whom we've imagined since we were small. However, our personal genie differs from the fairy tale or the Disney version. He, too, has incredible powers, but he won't drop pots of gold or doting lovers at our feet. Our genie, who is slavishly eager to serve us, is even more powerful. He's **The Man**—an endless source of creativity. Our genie is also jolly and wise and lots of fun. You don't need to learn a secret handshake or magic words or incantations to call him forth. Instead, writers and, indeed, everyone can summon the creativity genie merely by believing in him. Belief is so simple and yet so difficult.

How do we summon our genie? By consistent writing. The more we write, the more we write. Each time we sit at our computers or desks, the genie is signaled. It's so easy. He is summoned by the simple act of writing again and again. He is summoned by the power

of our routine, especially when we write at the same time each day. Just as Pavlov trained the laboratory dogs to salivate at the ringing of a bell, we can train our creativity to respond to our signal.

Think about how we respond to stimulus. It happens dozens of times each day since stimuli is everywhere. We flip on the television and watch a pizza commercial. It is a gooey, steamy invitation to cholesterol suicide. We know better; we planned on having a salad for dinner. But before you can say "extra pepperoni," we're digging in the refrigerator for a snack or dialing Domino's. We're responding to stimulus.

So we know that we're susceptible, that we're easy. That extra ten pounds we lug around is certainly proof. But there's also a positive side to working with stimulus. If we expect our creativity to respond every time we sit down to write, it will simply happen. The act of placing ourselves in our writing chair is the stimulus. Our right brain, the inspired, intuitive, unconscious part of us, responds to the stimulus of our writing routine. We sit down to form words, and the right brain is signaled, and ideas spin out of us like stars spattered against the night sky.

Approach your work confidently, yet relax, anticipating, trusting that your creativity is always at hand. Inspiration can't be beat into submission, it comes with letting go, with having faith. If you are attempting a short story, relax and let your mind wander. Find a memory. It doesn't have to be grand. Remember a hot summer day when you were ten, and flies buzzed in the thick air beyond the screen porch, and while you read comic books with the red-headed kid next door. Submerge yourself in the details, the textures of the memory. Soon the genie will blow sweet inspiration your way, and you'll be writing about two kids about to be kidnapped from their innocent play or kids who mastermind a scheme to steal their sister's diary.

Try imagining your genie—he's bald, wears gold earrings, is lime-green, 10-feet tall with an infectious laugh. Maybe he's got a Robin Williams personality like the Disney version. Or perhaps your genie is a female goddess-type: Athena beautiful and draped in garlands and veils. Creativity is easy, it's the magic in all of us. The genie is at your feet, call him. Believe.

try this

Find an object that symbolizes creativity and place it near your writing desk as a reminder that you are connected to an endless source. Maybe clouds or rainbows make you feel endlessly creative. Search for an evocative photograph of a shimmering rainbow or summer sky. Maybe you think that rose quartz holds infinite possibilities. Hang a Matisse print, a mandala, an African mask, a Shaker basket, a handmade quilt. Do fresh flowers inspire you? Throughout time it has been proven that symbols or totems have power to inspire us. Try it.

Immerse Yourself

"If you're a writer you locate yourself behind a wall of silence and no matter what you are doing, driving a car or walking or doing housework . . . you can still be writing, because you have that space."

Joyce Carol Oates

––––––––––––

When Peter Elbow wrote *Writing Without Teachers* and Natalie Goldberg wrote *Writing Down the Bones*, they proposed a whole new approach to writing. In fact, Elbow and Goldberg blew a fresh wind into the writer's repertoire of tricks and at the same time tossed out a lot of old constraints. They both preach the gospel of free-writing, that is, writing for a specific period of time when your pen doesn't stop moving. They both suggest that we write about nothing. Well, not exactly nothing, but free-writing or writing practice isn't about a specific **subject**; instead it involves a specific **process**.

Free-writing is designed to bring us to an easy, open access to our words within. As we skim our pen across the page, we're not focusing on the content or worrying about being perfect; we're simply putting down words.

The beauty of free-writing is the simple, unfettered flow of words. During free-writing, you don't worry about grammar, spelling, or punctuation. You just write. And you don't have to show it to anyone.

The reason for this exercise is simple. When we write without censoring ourselves, we bypass our critical left brain. The left brain is our censor, our critic, our editor. Sometimes it will stop our creative process before we have a chance to produce a single sentence.

Begin your writing day with a free-writing session. This is like a dancer stretching at the barre, a pianist playing scales, a singer vocalizing. Once you warm up with free writing, the rest of the writing flows better. Once we slip past the critical sensor, we develop confidence. We're inspired by the easy way the words pour out when we're not worrying about format. Ultimately, free-writing emancipates our voice and we write loose and fast and comfortably.

Along with free-writing, Goldberg recommends practice-writing. Sometimes we aren't ready to write a novel or break into a free-lance career. Instead, we practice to discover our voice, perfect our style. Or we practice writing simply because it's fun. It's challenging, but it doesn't count. We don't have to show it to an editor or our critique group. We write to find our way, to develop our own rhythm and nuance. We practice writing because the more we do it, the easier it gets. Practice gives us flow and confidence.

Sometimes writers don't practice because they don't know what to write about. Their minds are as blank as the sheet of paper in front of them. One solution lies in the collected images in our writer's notebook. Those keen observations we've been hoarding are a rich lode for writing topics. As we go through our days noticing everything, recording our memories and dreams, clipping bits from the newspaper, our notebooks become a source of inspiration. Having a cache of writing topics is another way to fight the blank-head syndrome. The topics are a nudge, a place to begin.

try this

Practice means writing without feeling pressured. Choose one of the topics listed here and write about it in your notebook. Remember, these practices don't count. They're about building muscles and confidence.

Write about the gardens in your neighborhood.

Write about your enemies.

Write abut the time you sensed an omen or a strong message in your life.

Write about your siblings—how do you really feel about them? Do your adult relationships mirror your childhood?

Write about your pets.

Write about a funeral you attended.

Write about your grandparents' houses.

Write about your childhood backyard.

Write about Saturdays when you were a kid.

Write about your favorite movies.

Write about food—describe pies, the challenge of rolling out pie crusts, the apples or berries bubbling out of a golden crust. Write about beef stew, lemons, broccoli, raspberries, pickles.

Write about your vacations or places you've visited.

Write about betrayal.

Write about the seasons. How do you respond to them? Be sure to include lots of sensory details.

Write about being sick.

Write a eulogy for yourself.

Write about a graveyard, a haunted house, a spooky cave.

Write about learning to ski, swim, bicycle, rollerblade, tango, rock climb, ice skate.

Write about shoes. What do they indicate about the wearers?

Write about waterfalls, rivers, lakes, the ocean.

Write about your favorite plants, flowers, trees.

Write about a secret you've always longed to reveal.

Write about what your religious/spiritual beliefs mean to you.

Write about music. Singing, jazz, classical, rock and roll—how does it move you? How has it enhanced your life?

Write a scene as though you are looking out a window—a train winding through the Rockies, a New York high rise, a farm kitchen, an airplane flying low.

Write about something that you've always been afraid to try.

Write about a favorite article of clothing. How does it make you feel to wear it?

Write about your body. What do you like or dislike about it?

Write about what your life is going to be like five, ten, fifteen, or twenty years from now.

Write about a miracle you've witnessed.

Write about babies.

Write about public places, churches, museums, parks, hospitals.

Write about holidays—what do they mean, how are they celebrated, what do your remember from your childhood?

Write about your dreams and nightmares.

Write about your ancestors. If you don't know them, invent some.

Write about the best or most moving experience you've had at a theatrical or musical performance.

Write about people you meet and for whom you form an instant dislike.

Write about accidents, injuries, near-death experiences.

Write About a Place

"The books that you really love give the sense, when you first open them, of having been there. It is a creation, almost like a chamber in the memory. Places that one has never been to, things that one has never seen or heard, but their fitness is so sound that you've been there somehow."

JOHN CHEEVER

Effective writing is filled with vivid sensory details. Writing about a place is great practice for beginning writers. As you record the specifics about a neighborhood, a campground, an English moor, the Rockies, breathe it into being so that a reader immediately has a sense of recognition. Search for the perfect details that bring a location to life, paint a dazzling picture. Exactly what color is the sky? Gun-metal gray? Azure? Lapis? What architectural styles do you see in your place? How about the weather, the climate, the sounds from nature? I once heard a novelist say that if he doesn't have a smell on every third page, that he goes back and puts one in. Remember to touch all the senses when you describe a place.

72

try this

Describe a place in detail. Add weather, clouds, insects, colors, and textures. Take your reader with you so that he or she can smell the salt air, be baked by the desert heat, or chilled in the haunted chill of an old mansion.

Describe:

A World War II submarine.

An inner-city drug house.

An ocean shore.

The Mojave Desert.

A lush wine region, like Burgundy, Bordeaux, Napa.

A Portuguese fishing village.

A Midwest farm.

A tropical island.

A maple-sugar camp in the spring while the sap is processed.

A detention camp in Poland or Germany in 1943.

A giant aquarium like the Shedd Aquarium in Chicago.

An English village in 1918.

An Irish village during the potato famine.

An old, abandoned mansion still filled with dust-covered furniture and mementos.

Write About Conflict

"Somebody gets into trouble, gets out of it. People love that story. They never get tired of it."

Kurt Vonnegut

What is conflict? In fiction, conflict is the glue that binds the story. Conflict provides the tension that keeps the reader involved. Conflict represents the obstacles and struggles faced by the protagonist. It means being pulled in two directions, impaled on the horns of a dilemma. Conflict can be a rite of passage, a realization, a challenge, a tragedy. Conflict makes the characters battle, look inward, and grow. Without conflict, there is no fiction.

Even if we don't write fiction, however, we know about conflict. Some girls play the familiar game of plucking daisy petals while chanting, "he loves, he loves me not, he loves me, he loves me not." Conflict marks most of our days—we want too many things, and we can't squeeze all our dreams into our hectic schedules. We have to make hard choices. Conflict often feels lousy, makes us doubt ourselves. Our friend is faced with the terrible decision—she must make arrangements to place her ailing father in a nursing home, because the family can no longer care for him. But, her father hates nursing homes, wants to keep living at home although the whole family is worn and weary. Parents are forced to discipline their children when they're not sure how to handle the issues at hand. Conflict is a part of ordinary life with all its dissonance, discord, and decisions.

try this

Portray conflict for the following characters. Ask yourself about the choices and problems that they face.

A worker on an assembly line.

A battered wife.

A preacher who's lost his faith.

A man or woman who's discovered his or her spouse has a lover.

A corporate mogul who must fire his second-in-command.

A pilot who's about to take a plane up but is not feeling up to par.

A person dying of AIDs.

An aging, ailing dancer, writer, artist.

A writer who's written one great novel but can't summon the creativity for another.

A child who is forced to choose his/her custodial parent during a divorce.

A psychic who loses his/her gift to "see."

Writing is Therapeutic

"You get a great deal off your chest—emotions, impressions, opinions. Curiosity urges you on—the driving force. What is collected must be got rid of. That's one thing to be said about writing. There is a great sense of relief in a fat volume."

JOHN DOS PASSOS

It is October. Last night as I walked to my car after teaching, the autumn air stung my cheeks. And this morning, although the sun has finally broken through the Portland sky, it doesn't warm me through. For the third day in a row, a flock of Canadian geese has honked past, heading south. Like many writers, I love autumn because it signals the beginning of the school year. I am in love with learning, ideas, books.

Each season has a different perspective. Summer is probably the hardest time to write because the weather demands that we linger outdoors. Our gardens call, mountain trails and campgrounds beg us to return. Spring is a yearly miracle we want to witness up close, of daffodils and soft green hues and lilac scents lingering on sweet air. Winter has its subtle charms. In this part of the world, they are mostly wet and gray. Still, the deep, mysterious winter clouds of the Pacific Northwest make me think we live in a wet, island world, separate from reality. We are perched on the edge of the country, squeezed between ocean and mountains, and here the land wants all the rain it can lap up.

Through all this we write.

We write as the earth swings in its mysterious rotation. We write as our hair grays, our friends betray us, our children grow, our families lose touch. We write as the candle flickers across the face of our beloved, our children wrap their love in a homemade card, our friends rally around when we are afraid.

There is so much richness in our lives, it would be a shame not to record all we can. In our personal journals we record the gray hairs and missed steps and children leaving

home. In our writers' journals we note the geese flying past, the moods of sunlight in different seasons, the mystery of night sky, the flowers blooming, fading, withering.

The more I write, the healthier I am. I know myself more deeply. I know the world more deeply. I am at once in touch with myself at every age that I remember and involved in the spinning planet around me.

The more I write, the more empathy I have. With my family, friends, strangers on the street. I see us all as pieces of a wonderful mystery for which there are no clear answers. Yet in the midst of unanswered questions, there is dignity and caring and connection.

The more I write, the more courage I have. I believe in my ability to find the right words. I learn that I am infinitely creative, able to discover solutions to life's problems and plot twists.

The more I write, the simpler my life becomes. Dramas and struggles and tragedies diminish as I put this process first. My role in life is to love as many people as I can; but my calling is to record these loves in some form.

The more I write, the more I believe in myself. If I have finally mastered this form of self-expression and can teach it to others, I know I am okay. I know I will always triumph because I triumph daily at my keyboard.

try this

Write about the worst day of your life. Was it the day your mother died, your child ran away from home, you were attacked by a stranger or beaten by your father? Now return to this hideous memory and rewrite the incident so that you triumph over the pain, reconcile with your child, chase off the attacker, stand down your father.

Write When You're Miserable

"One must be pitiless about this matter of 'mood.' In a sense the writing will create the mood. If art is, as I believe it to be, a genuinely transcendental function—a means by which we rise out of limited, parochial states of mind—then it should not matter very much what states of mind or emotion we are in. Generally, I've found this to be true: I have forced myself to begin writing when I've been utterly exhausted, when I've felt my soul as thin as a playing-card, when nothing has seemed worth enduring for another five minutes . . . and somehow the activity of writing changes everything. Or appears to do so."

JOYCE CAROL OATES

Some years ago I was experiencing a series of crises and losses so hideous I wasn't sure I'd survive the pain. But survive I did, and eventually time started erasing the blunt edges of loss, and new friendships filled empty hours. My biggest mistake while I was going through this turmoil was not writing enough while I was in the midst of it.

There are times when life blows us far from our course, when it's hard to claim a life raft of safety and calm from which we can write. No matter how strong the storm, how far we drift, we write anyway. When the black shadow of loneliness swoops into your life, write about it. When the yawning ache of lost love is all you can think about, write instead. Transform the sting of rejection or the misery of illness by writing about it.

Write when you gain weight or lose favor with your boss. Write when you hurt your back or fall in love. Write when you've missed your train, lost your keys, ruined your favorite sweater in the wash, gotten a lousy haircut.

Write when you feel like weeping, giving up, strangling your spouse, hitting your child. Write when you can't sleep, when you can't pay your bills, when you want to run away from home.

I guarantee that in the midst of sorrow, loss, or pain writing can be the ultimate solace. Writing can be the safe place, the shoulder on which to cry, the analyst's couch. Writing can help us realize how powerful it is to go inside ourselves for strength. Writing can be the normalizing routine in the storm of crisis, the cup of hot tea on a bitter night.

Write when you're sad. Write when you've lost your way. Write when you've lost faith in your ability to write.

Little by little, the pain will loosen its death grip, the crisis will start to resolve. Writing can't solve all our problems, but writing can be a sure method of coping.

Sit down and start writing.

try this

Stop longing and waiting for the perfect mood to strike. Learn how to write despite your moods. The next time a dilemma or crisis occurs, take the time to write about it. Practice writing from another perspective as if someone older, wiser, and calmer were describing your problem. Imagine that the outcome doesn't matter, that the problem is happening to someone else or the issue is happily resolved.

Write about small blessings, treasures, and comforts. Write about hot chocolate with marshmallows, straw hats, down quilts, spring flowers, sleeping late on weekends, mountain meadows, bubble baths, back rubs, naps, holding babies, and new shoes.

Whole Brain Strategies

"The aim of art is to represent not the outward appearance of things, but their inward significance; for this, and not the external mannerism and detail, is true reality."

<small>ARISTOTLE</small>

There are two distinct steps in writing. The first step is the quick, intuitive putting down of words. The second is rewriting or editing, honing and polishing the words until they are just right. Each of these processes relies on different hemispheres of the brain. The unconscious, creative side of our brain is the right side, and we rely on it for our first drafts. The critical, analytical side of the brain is the left, and we use these skills when we edit and rewrite.

The left brain: corrects mistakes, "male," logical, rational, censor, sequential thought. The right brain: original, "female," intuitive, unconventional, sensory, insight, design-oriented.

The right brain is childlike, enthralled by new ideas, seeing the world with eyes of wonder. The left brain is the adult, pulling us back with exhortations to get it right. The left hemisphere give us actual access to the language and orderly thought. The right empowers us with sensory images, flow, metaphor, rhythm, and emotions. The left hemisphere likes one-at-a-time processes; the right hemisphere sees the world all at once, sees connections and wholeness.

Writers are most productive when they enhance the powers of the right brain, silencing the left hemisphere critic, accomplishing the important task of first-draft writing.

Free-writing exercises, writing quickly without interference from the left brain, is a great a way to access the right side of the brain. As we free-write, we write with abandon. We hit our stride, learn to trust ourselves and our creative capabilities.

Another method of tapping into the right brain is clustering or mind mapping. Clustering is a fabulous method for brain storming ideas and getting unstuck. The technique is simple: Start with a noun, a concept, or a character. If possible, choose a word that has some heat or an emotional spark. On a clean sheet of paper, write this word in the center, as a nucleus, then draw a circle around it. Now, as quickly as possible, jot down other words that spring to mind when you consider the nucleus word. The words or ideas that follow should be arranged like a constellation of circles around the nucleus.

The key to clustering is forming words in a pattern so that the right brain can conceive the connections between ideas. Clustering keeps the censoring left brain out of the brainstorming process. Clustering allows your innate, creative voice to have its say. It releases the genie within.

Your clusters will resemble wagon spokes or a lopsided configuration. You will attach the new words that emerge to the original, nuclear word with lines, resembling spokes on a bicycle or sun rays in children's drawings. Circle each of the new words. If several words have a similar meaning, join them along a line like the body of a caterpillar. When a new train of thought occurs, draw a separate line from the nucleus.

Spend five, ten, fifteen minutes working on this design. Next, take another sheet of paper and write, using the inspirations located in your clustering design. You'll discover that the writing that follows clustering is spontaneous and clear.

Clustering is a way to break through the I-don't-know-how-to-start resistance that beginning writers experience. It takes you beyond fear through a playful process into the writing process.

Sue Grafton writes a series of mystery novels based on a female private detective, Kinsey Milhone. Her fans have followed Kinsey's exploits through more than a dozen books. Critical readers of Grafton's series notice that Grafton's voice and technique is becoming deeper and clearer, that she is growing as a writer. I am convinced that much of Grafton's power comes from her deep belief in her right brain's capabilities.

One of her tricks is to call on her right brain to solve a writing problem before she goes to bed at night. She believes that sleep loosens the hold of the left brain and allows the right brain to find solutions. These answers don't always occur in her dreams, but she finds that often, when she awakes, a particular problem is resolved.

For every novel that Grafton writes, she also keeps a writing journal. The journal is integral to her work methods and often becomes longer than the novel. Her journal becomes a clearing-house for ideas and a place to record her right brain answers for the novel. The journal fills with free-writing, details from everyday life, her worries about the book, her insecurities. This practice allows her to deal with the emotional aspects of life so the slate is cleared for the deeper work of fiction writing. Whenever she feels stuck, she returns to her journal pages and finds reflections that ultimately help her with the novel.

Another trick that Grafton uses is writing notes to her right brain. The notes go something like this: *Dear Right Brain, I've asked you for help with this special place in the book. Please come through tonight and solve this problem. Your friend, Sue.* Grafton believes that the right brain likes these little notes and, within a few days, gives her the answer.

Free-writing, journal-writing, clustering, asking for answers before sleep—these are all tricks to tap into the creative right brain. If the right brain is allowed the freedom to operate fully, our words and ideas will pour out.

try this

Borrow Sue Grafton's trick of communicating with your right brain. What will you ask for? How will you talk to your right brain? Will you leave notes for your right brain or write in a journal? How about asking your dreams for information, inspiration, answers?

Write With Heat

"There are significant moments in everyone's day that can make literature. That's what you ought to write about."

RAYMOND CARVER

———————————

When we are in the midst of good writing, the world fades away. We can't write fast enough, our fingers almost slip off the keyboard, or grow numb with pain from clutching a pen for hours. We write because we must. The words hold us in their spell. This heat, this flow, this golden moment shouldn't be taken lightly. When the thrill of connecting with words hits, surrender to it and put down the words as fast as they come. As in freewriting, don't worry about the fine points. Later, iron out the grammar and spelling. For now, get close to the emotion and let it pour out like water tumbling down a mountain stream.

Beginning writers should write about subjects that they're passionate about. Then we're guaranteed a passion, a connection with the subject that will pull words out of us. Write close to the bone, near your heart. Write about loneliness, desperate empty moments, hungers, deep longings. We are formed and tested by pain, so don't be afraid to visit those dark corners.

Write about how you always hungered for acceptance, but were the last kid selected for the dodge-ball game. How you were afraid of dogs, deep water, climbing trees, while the rest of the kids in the neighborhood seemed to skim along, oblivious. Record your first menstrual period, the awkwardness of a constantly changing body. Write about how you always wanted to be pretty, but were born with a big nose, a funny butt, and wiry, strange hair. Remember your weird cousins and your grandfather's gall bladder surgery. And by all means write a few paragraphs about the classroom bully who spit in your face. And the shame-filled nights you wet the bed. Make yourself laugh and cry and blush, remembering these delicious, pain-filled details. Then put it down on paper.

Go for the good stuff, and slip into all your joys and triumphs. Remember your baby's smiles and tender lovers, perfect soufflés and hitting the high notes. Write about parking karma and beach vacations. Dredge up that perfect afternoon in San Francisco and how you danced until the wee hours on your fortieth birthday. Remember the time you won the soap box derby, hit the winning home run, and the prettiest girl asked you to dance. Our lives are jewels. Gratitude makes us aware, give us endless topics to write about.

I once taught a writing class for a group of young men who were dying of AIDs. Aware of how little time remained, they wanted to leave their stories for their friends and families. I noticed that since they didn't have the luxury of procrastination, they wrote the essentials, shared themselves wholly on the page. Their writing was true and brutal and scary and beautiful.

Write as if you are dying and must tell all your stories before you pass on.

Write fast, then put it away. Don't start editing immediately. Let it rest. Preferably let it rest overnight, then come back to it the following day with fresh eyes. It doesn't matter if we understand how these unconscious processes work; it's enough to believe that sleep reshapes our words. The deeper layers of creativity and unconsciousness work unfettered while the conscious mind is resting.

After you awake, return to the first draft and start editing. First, fill in the gaps; next prune, weed, polish, embellish. Then put it away again and sleep on it another night.

Come back the next day with another fresh perspective. How does it look? Still wordy? Unclear? Polish some more. If possible, sleep on the second draft and edit a final time the next day. Leaving time between our drafts improves them immensely. Of course, a lot of print journalists don't have this luxury. Deadlines demand fast writing, and the faster they write and edit the more successful they'll be. However, editing three or four times is ideal for those of us with the luxury of time before the editor beckons.

No matter how experienced an editor you are, the first draft is the most important. Write fearlessly, write passionately, tell the whole truth.

try this

Write about your secrets. What have you never told your closest friends, your spouse? Does your family share a secret? How do secrets make you feel? Ashamed? Sad? Conspiratorial?

The Inner Voice

"You must become aware of the richness in you and come to believe in
it and know it is there, so that you can write opulently and with self-trust.
If you become aware of it and have faith in it, you will be all right."

BRENDA UELAND

We are all called to wisdom by our inner voice. This inner voice whispers, beckons, pokes, nudges, admonishes, if we will only pause to pay attention. The inner voice, our intuition, can be an invaluable help for writers willing to trust and listen. My definition of true maturity is when we finally stop silencing our inner voice and start allowing it to guide us.

What is the inner voice? Our intuition, advisor, guidance, our inner counselor.

Sometimes when we hear the inner voice speaking, it's like hearing the sounds of our own voice chattering inside our head. Sometimes it's a mere whisper, a warning, a nagging sensation that we can't dismiss, yet have no words for. Sometimes it's a brilliant flash of insight. Sometimes it's a physical sensation—a tingling, a pull in our gut. Often it's a sudden burst of energy or a lightening-quick decision or solution. Our inner voice might appear as movies or images in our head with us playing a starring role. We can experience our inner voice through coincidences or omens. At times we sense the inner voice in a physical way, as a clutch of fear in our stomach or a tingling along our neck or spine.

What does this have to with writing?

Writing is a lifelong journey of discovery. Paying attention to our inner voice is an essential leg of the journey. The inner voice lives deep in our core being and is a link, a connection to a creative, guiding source. Some of us think that the inner voice is God whispering to us. When we become acquainted with our inner self, we bring depth and wisdom to our writing. Listening to the inner voice means learning to trust our instincts and lean on our source of inspiration. This can guide us in our writing as well as our actions.

Think about the times when you heeded the small warnings from within. Remember the consequences of ignoring or obeying the inner voice. Were you wise? Did you listen?

Don't confuse the inner voice with fear. They are not the same. Fear is a learned response to real or imagined danger. Intuition is our deep, wise self that will help us with all our struggles and creative projects.

"New Age" philosophies recommend that we "align" with our inner voice. When we align our cars, they run smoother, they don't pull to the right, or rattle when we cruise the highway. Aligning with our inner voice also makes our life run smoother.

The most basic aligning technique is to sit down and write when the urge overtakes us. Sometimes an idea pops in unannounced, but we ignore it or postpone recording it. If we don't jot down these insights, they will weaken or disappear. Inspiration strikes at inconvenient moments—while we're in traffic or under the shower, but it's important to pay homage to our insight. The more often you pause to hear it, record it, then act on it, the more often the inner voice will send you inspiration.

Imagine your inner voice as a league of invisible advisors that hover near. They are knowing, concerned, and patient. The only way they can communicate is through small whisperings, so you must become willing, train your ears. Tune in. If you ignore the voice, you ignore your power and guidance system. And they're on your side. Listen.

try this

Recall the times when you followed your intuition. What happened? Remember the times when you ignored your intuition. What were the results? Can you make an analogy for your intuition? Is it like inner weather? Does your awareness remind you of distant thunder? A tugging in your gut? Start tracking your intuitive insights in your writer's notebook. Can you spot any patterns?

Get A Life

*"Here's a major point of tension in most writer's lives: How can we rub
enough with the world to nourish our writing, while keeping the world
enough at bay to safeguard our creative energies?"*

FRANCINE DU PLESSIX GRAY

Writers aren't monks, although monks can be writers. Forget harsh vows of poverty, chastity, and dullness. Many writers would be better writers if they'd just get a life. Writers need input, involvement; they need to be alert and interested in the world around them.

I remember one of my first news reporting classes in college. The teacher was a retired journalist, and every Monday she scheduled a current events quiz. At first I didn't take her seriously, but after I flunked a few quizzes, I began studying the daily papers and paying attention to every newscast. By the end of the semester, I knew about sports standings, disasters, international political figures, and local political issues. My instructor claimed that you could only be a decent journalist if you were aware of the world around you. She was right.

Whenever I read a book by a young author that is full of heart and depth and wisdom, I wonder how he or she pulled it off, because I think there is a direct relationship to good writing and good living. The longer and better we live, the more insight we bring to our writing. Older writers have advantages: experience, depth, discernment.

Our writing is enhanced by critical reading, but it's also enhanced by all the arts. Writers should attend concerts, movies, theater, readings, performances.

Forget about a solitary existence. Writers need friends of all types and backgrounds. Writers need adventures, vacations, camping trips, family reunions.

Writers should read biographies, novels, children's books, books about writing techniques, screenplays, best sellers, news magazines, Sunday newspapers, trade magazines.

Read works by the Pulitzer and Nobel prize winners, short-story anthologies, literary quarterlies and classics. Read a variety of magazines. Magazines are contemporary examinations of society. The editors and advertisers know their readers. What do the magazines tell us about culture, psychology, trends?

Although this advice might sound trite, I'll offer it anyway: writers are lifelong students. Study history, politics, economics, art, anatomy. Anything. Don't ever stop learning and growing. Admit there's never enough time to study all the mysteries of this twirling planet, so sandwich bits of knowledge into each day. I like to read when I eat alone, when my students are working in class, while I soak in the tub, before bed, when I'm ill.

Listen to public radio, alternative radio, and AM-radio talk shows. Sort the trash from the wisdom, the rant from the substance, and keep listening. Watch specials on Public Television such as *Masterpiece Theater*. Most television programs waste our time and don't challenge our intellect, so I never advise writers to watch TV. Television isn't about life. Television imitates life and usually does it badly. If you spend a lot of time in front of the tube, reclaim those precious hours for writing or reading.

There are many myths about the writing life. One is that the writer must isolate himself, take up a drab, monastic routine. This myth has its roots in stereotypes and truths: the lonely writer's garret, the solitary struggle to put words to paper. We know that most writing is done alone. This is indisputable. And there are a few harsh realities that go hand-in-hand with the writing life style. You'll likely have less time for fun than your friends who work normal nine to five hours. Sometimes you'll have to turn down invitations. In fact, some of these invitations will be tantalizing and too good to be true. With a sinking heart, you'll watch your friends leave for weekends at the beach, and you'll feel orphaned as you slump back to work at your lonely computer. Maybe you'll resent your friends' smug lives, or maybe you won't, since you're too busy reveling in your marvelous flow of words. But chances are, being a writer sometimes will cause you to miss out on fun.

However, a warning here: don't turn down every invitation. Writers must be well-rounded, involved in community and celebrations. Loners do not make the best writers. Art and friendship feed our spirits and ultimately our words. A writer needs laughter and dinner parties that linger over a last bottle of wine while candles flicker on the faces of those we love. Writers need kids to hang out with so that we can nurture them—and remind us of who we used to be. Go out into the world, feed your head. Don't put off living a full life to be a writer.

try this

List all the joys in your life. Do you love hiking, gardening, dancing the tango, attending the opera? Include the small joys in your list, too: reading in the bathtub, sitting near a fire, sleeping on fresh, cotton sheets, watering your houseplants, painting your toenails, washing your car. Are you making time for at least three of these items each week?

Set Goals

"How we spend our days is, of course, how we spend our lives. What we do with this hour, and that one, is what we are doing. A schedule defends from chaos and whim. It is a net for catching days. It is a scaffolding on which a worker can stand and labor with both hands at sections of time. A schedule is a mock-up of reason and order—willed, faked, and so brought into being; it is a peace and a haven set into the wreck of time; it is a lifeboat on which you find yourself, decades later, still living. Each day is the same, so you remember the series afterward as a blurred and powerful pattern."

ANNIE DILLARD

By now, you've realized that it's one thing to claim that you're a writer, while it's quite another to actually pursue your writing dreams. Real writers set real goals, while wannabe writers drift, blather on about some day.

The more precise and specific the goals, the better. We all need guidelines to keep our butts in our writing chair. It just doesn't work to proclaim that you're going to become a writer if you haven't developed a specific plan of action.

First, concoct a dream list. Write down all the projects you'd like to write in the next few years, beginning with the big ones such as a column, novel, screenplay, poetry collection. Now, start thinking about smaller projects, articles, query letters, short stories.

Consider all your writing goals. Do you need to develop a filing system or a Rolodex of publishing contacts? Do you need to subscribe to writing magazines? How about entering contests? Arranging an office space to work in? Upgrading your equipment? Maybe you should attend a writing class or a workshop taught by a professional writer. Take time to make a thoughtful inventory of your writing system.

Now go back to that dream list. First of all, forget about working on just one project at a time. Writing is easier if you are working on several ongoing projects of varying lengths and complexities. If the writing in one project gets bogged down, it helps to slip

over to another one, to revive yourself there. I like to have at least one book in process and two or three shorter projects to choose from.

I recommend that you set two kinds of goals. First, decide how many hours per week you can realistically set aside for writing. I suggest eight hours as a minimum for people with full-time jobs. Ideally, if you're serious about a writing career, you should spend at least twenty or more hours a week at your craft.

We've all heard tales of mythical free-lance writers who work seventy or eighty hours a week. We can't imagine that we'll ever be able to spend that many hours on the job. Don't let these Herculean schedules scare you. Start anywhere. Fifteen minutes in the morning, half an hour at lunch, an hour before bedtime. But remember: Your writing time is sacred. It is your commitment to your future and to the child within who dreamed of writing glory. Honor your personal commitment, and watch the words pile up.

Next, decide the number of pages you'll complete each month. Two or three pages a day means that you'll complete sixty to ninety pages per month, a respectable output. You could easily finish a book in a year if you wrote two or three pages every day.

Don't set yourself up for failure. You won't write like Hemingway, Styron, or your favorite literary hero when you start out. Hemingway and Styron started at the bottom, too, doubting themselves, collecting rejections. Like you, they had to pay their dues and develop a personal style. Find a mentor or a role model whom you admire. Examine your literary hero's style and incorporate some of his or her techniques into your work. List the characteristics of their writing that you admire and decide how you're going to emulate them. Go beyond their writing style, research their work habits, their path to success. I'm not advising plagiarism here; I'm suggesting that you mimic another writer's strengths, while you discover your own. Remember that every writer starts at the same place, undiscovered, unsure, yet burning with a desire to write.

Start small. Modest, achievable goals work the best. It's important to finish something, anything. Completion brings accomplishment, which fuels courage. Forget about writing the Great American Novel. Forget about your lofty plans for the Pulitzer prize and making your mother proud. These goals frighten us and stifle our words. Instead, write a letter to an editor or a distant friend, a song, a perfect paragraph, a lively page, a poem, a journal entry, a short story. When you feel ready for bigger and bolder projects, outline the plot for a novel. Or draft a plan for writing your memoirs.

Re-evaluate your goals every few months. Are your goals realistic? Are you able to pick up the pace and double your time at the computer? Is there a stronger flow to your writing so that you can produce more words at a faster pace? Don't be afraid to push harder, expect more from yourself.

Successful writers plan far ahead. Consider listing your five- or ten-year goals, your lifetime goals. Inspire yourself: plan a lifetime of accomplishment.

Finally, keep your goals in front of you where you'll see them daily, a constant reminder to spur yourself through doubt or sluggish output.

try this

In your writer's notebook list all the times that you set goals, then followed through and accomplished them. As you make this list, remember your childhood and recall your earliest accomplishments and successes. Now, track your greatest achievement. What was your first step? How did you manage your time? Did anyone help you? Can you transfer any of these skills and apply them to your writing goals?

Discipline

"Discipline is a bad word in our culture. People associate it with having to do what they're told. But discipline is quite a lovely word. It comes from the same root as disciple, and it means seeing yourself through the eyes of a teacher who loves you. We have the teacher within ourselves; we also have the wild animal that needs to be disciplined with love. We need all its instinctual energy and wisdom."

MARION WOODMAN

Writers are a rare breed, made up of one part creative force, one part discipline, one part courage. In my writing classes there are two kinds of students; good writers and bad writers. Yet they both have an equal chance of making it. Why? Because natural ability doesn't mean much; persistence and discipline are the keys to success.

Writing happens alone. There is no support staff, boss, water-cooler gossip, 401K plan, or car pool. Most of us work at home. It is lonely, solitary. There are no quarterly goals laid down by your supervisor, no raises when you land a big account, no praise when you finish a project. The discipline to write, to keep at it, comes from within.

All of my life I was convinced that I wasn't disciplined. That I was a dreamer, not a doer. That other people achieved their goals, while I talked about mine. Along the way I've changed these beliefs. Hour after hour, day after day, I sit at my computer and punch in words. Sometimes the words are marvelous, sometimes the words are weak, ineffectual. I know it doesn't matter as long as I carve out the time to do it.

Discipline. Persistence. Courage.

There are no vitamins that provide these characteristics. They are not genetic traits. These characteristics are invisible, but they mean everything.

If you aren't brave, determined, and stubborn, give up the dream of writing. Dreams aren't enough.

We all need an inner drill sergeant, coach, or personal trainer exhorting us to write. If need be, he grabs us by our ear and pushes us into our writing chair and forces us to stay until we've accomplished our goals. He has bad breath and a raspy, grating voice, and he carries a thick club to smack our desk for emphasis when we don't pay attention.

In other words, he scares us into being good.

But is it really being good that we're talking about here? Or is it just being good to ourselves? Discipline isn't a dirty word. It's satisfying to have a routine, goals, desires. It's fun to write essays, fiction, poetry, or songs.

Or maybe you prefer a gentler approach, say, an inner angel. She cajoles us to do our best. She leads us by the hand, gently presses us into our writing chair, and kneads our shoulders while we struggle over the keyboard. Our writing angel showers us in praise and adulation when we finish a page. Under her soft ministrations we leap out of bed each morning, eager to please her. She rewards us lavishly and loves us unconditionally, so that we gladly labor hard and long. Work is transformed to a higher calling.

No matter which model of discipline you choose, you must find a method that works for you.

Discipline means finding your inner master.

Discipline means squashing the saboteur.

Discipline means not being afraid of failure.

Discipline means writing despite laziness and bad habits.

Discipline means writing anyway when you want weep with frustration.

Discipline means writing anyway when you want to toss your computer out the window and then jump out after it.

There are a lot of talented writers in the world, but there are not nearly enough writers who persist; who carve out a routine, set goals, and persevere; who discover the rewards of discipline.

try this

Describe your strengths. Are you a good listener? Are you compassionate, patient, spontaneous, slow to anger, forgiving, resilient, ambitious, kind?

Describe how you've used your strengths to achieve your goals. Did you join a gym and work out four times a week until you changed your body-fat ratio? Did you attend a parenting class so that you could be a better mother? Did you give up alcohol, chocolate, meat, dairy products, or cigarettes? Did you teach yourself a computer program? Did you learn to speak Italian? Did you master tai chi? Tennis? Tap dancing? Tango?

Write Past the Silence

"A writer's life is about examination. What is love anyway, and sorrow, and light? I wasn't ready to examine those things for their own sake. I was busy examining myself. How do I get this mind to speak clearly, how do I coordinate it with my hand and pen, who is a writer, how do I become one?"

NATALIE GOLDBERG

Sometimes despite our best intentions, we have nothing to say. The writing is flat, uninspired, even insipid. Or there are no words at all. We hate ourselves, we hate our life. We're convinced we have no talent, that we should have become a plumber, an architect, anything but a writer. We strive for words and find a yawning, horrible silence.

You must write past the silence.

It doesn't matter how you do it, but don't let that void grow. Once you give in to this silence, it deepens and grows and like a tumor, it takes over. If you become stuck while writing a novel, the place where you're stuck will erode into a hole as each day of silence passes. After a while, this hole will turn into a canyon, and, if the canyon deepens, it will become bottomless, until, sadly, you put the book into a drawer with the rest of your unfinished works.

Find a place to break the silence. It doesn't matter where. Many novelists get stuck in the middle. Go back to the beginning and edit in order to resume the flow of your ideas. Write the ending and work your way back. Write letters or converse with your characters. Write biographies for your character's family, describe their home, their wardrobes, the contents of their refrigerator. Get closer, know them better. Sometimes when we write fiction, we become stuck because we are not well acquainted with our characters.

Sometimes we can't write because we're convinced our writing is no good. Find a best seller and examine it thoroughly. Analyze how and why it works, the techniques that the author employs with success. Next write another chapter as if it belongs in the book, mimicking the author's voice and style. If you're still stuck, try another author on for size, all the while examining his or her style closely. Again, imitate this author's voice. If you still have doubts, find a bad novel; there are plenty of them. Rewrite and improve the novelist's junk until something wonderful emerges. Keep at these exercises until you stumble out of the silence and confidence starts creeping in.

Sometimes we can't write because our life is in shambles. People we love hurt us, leave us, betray us. Write about betrayal, loss, divorce, pain. Don't let pain stop your writing. Writing will help put the pain in perspective. Write letters that you don't send. Write letters to yourself when you were ten years old. Write letters to your best friend in second grade. Write descriptions of your fourth-grade classroom. Write about your best vacation, the time you almost drowned, the time you saw your boyfriend kiss another girl.

Write a commercial, a joke, a recipe, an editorial, a song, a description of your kitchen. It doesn't matter what you write; what matters is that you don't allow the silence to take over. This isn't a comforting, restful silence we're talking about. This silence is the enemy, and, like any enemy, it is deadly and must be confronted.

try this

Borrow a beginning. Jump into a story by taking off after the first line:
My sister Greta was destined for trouble. This was obvious to us all when she _____
The night the UFO landed in our backyard I found out that _____
Edith was the kind of girl who learned early that _____
When I was fourteen and babysitting for my Aunt Lou and Uncle Bill, I was always in a hurry to tuck my younger cousins into bed so that I could spend time with Uncle Bill's porn collection. After all these years I haven't forgotten_____
When I was a kid, it was just plain stupid to tell_____
After Alice, the elephant rampaged through the Big Top, trampled the side shows and tore past the _____ , bellowing all the way, all I could do was stand by helplessly and hope that_____
It was obvious to everyone that ever met him, that Roger was born to suffer.

Keep An Idea File

"The books that you really love give the sense, when you first open them, of having been there. It is a creation, almost like a chamber in the memory. Places that one has never been to, things that one has never seen or heard, but their fitness is so sound that you've been there somehow."

JOHN CHEEVER

Have you ever had a terrible craving, say for chocolate ice cream, then, for some reason, couldn't have it? No matter the reason—it was two in the morning, pouring rain, or you needed to lose ten pounds, and, tragically, your hunger went unanswered. Maybe you opted for a peanut butter and jelly sandwich instead. The sandwich filled the empty spot in your stomach but didn't soothe the appetite. You still wanted chocolate—bad.

Sometimes writing is like that. You want to write something sinfully rich, sumptuous, wonderful. But the cupboard is bare. Some days I have four or five projects before me to work on. And then there are the days when nothing appeals. I'm just not inspired, writing is a yawn, a drag, a painful duty. I'm hungry, but my appetite has turned finicky.

If you're involved with your writing goals, you've been keeping a writer's journal or notebook. This journal sustains you during lean times, sorts out complex issues, examines the pains and joys of the writing process. Sometimes, during starvation times, our writer's journal provides an idea that jump-starts stalled creativity and has us off and writing. Then again, sometimes the journal just doesn't fit the bill.

For these lean times I keep idea files. I fill the files regularly and faithfully and regularly review them.

What do I put in the files? Just about anything that strikes my interest. My first file is labeled food-writing ideas. Recipes, menus, tips, articles about diets, nutrition, chefs' advice, edible flowers, herbs, and clippings about cooking techniques.

I also write about wine and have an extensive wine file. My wine files are organized by wine regions and varieties. The file bulges with maps of wine regions, public relations materials from wine associations, clippings from magazines and newspapers, wine columns, recipes, quotes from wine experts, wine-tasting notes.

My third file is a general catch-all, jammed with articles and ideas I've clipped from newspapers and magazines. It holds book reviews, quotes, articles about life styles, trends, farmers' markets, micro-breweries, get-away weekends, bookstores. I collect photographs of intriguing faces to inspire development of fictional characters. Sometimes these overheard quotes or faces from real life fit my fictional characters or inspire an essay or short story.

Idea files are fun and a valuable tool for beginning writers, a resource, a cupboard that's never bare. It doesn't matter if you write fiction or nonfiction; all writing springs from somewhere, and clipping files are a cheap source of inspiration.

try this

Start an idea file. Collect columns, quotes, articles, reviews and photographs. Trace your interests and intrigues. Have you always wanted to write about Argentina? Are you fascinated with UFOs, cowboy poetry, glass blowing, Belgian lace, Shakers, wedding photographers, bowling, gardening, Nepal, football statistics, Spike Lee's career?

Don't Wait For Your Family

"The role of the writer is not to say what we can all say, but what we are unable to say."

ANAÏS NIN

We've all read dedication pages in the front of books gushing with thanks to the writers' spouses or families. Undoubtedly, these dedications are heartfelt and genuine. Yet, according to my experience and those of writers I know, you can't count on your family to support your writing. If they do, that's great. If they don't, write anyway.

Ideally, we enlist the support of our family in our goals and dreams. For those of us with children, lacking the support of our partner, we'll never attain our goals. Do whatever is necessary; beg, grovel, plead, or offer bribes for his or her cooperation and understanding. But at the same time, stand firm and explain that your writing is essential to your well-being. Insist that your writing space is hallowed, that the time you spend sweating over your novel or article is not to be interrupted unless the house catches fire or another crisis worthy of a 9-1-1 call occurs.

Repeat your rules as often as necessary, and, although your kids plead with you to join them in the living room to watch television reruns, don't give in to temptation. Even if they dangle hot buttered popcorn in front of your nose. Even if your novel is going nowhere and it's your favorite John Travolta movie. Keep writing. Keep repeating to yourself and your family that your writing comes first. They'll get the message.

A word of caution. I don't advocate that you ignore your family until you make it as a writer. I'm not suggesting that your children exist on peanut butter and jelly sandwiches for the entire year that it takes you to finish the novel. Nor do I advise you to stop telling bedtime stories or attending parent-teacher conferences or making love. Include your family in your goals. Set aside specific times for family activities and faithfully participate. *After* you've sculpted your writing routine.

Then there is an even thornier issue; sometimes our families simply don't want us to write. They think that writing is silly, frivolous, that there is no money in it. They protest that we have a perfectly good job, and we should stick with it. Your spouse suggests that you sell plumbing parts, your father-in-law wants you to join the family business. Remain firm, calm, resolute as you refuse **their** plans for **your** life. Write anyway.

Often their lack of support stems from other reasons. Many families are uncomfortable with having a writer among them because they don't want us to tell the truth. This reluctance might stem from your parents, siblings, spouse, children. On some level, they're threatened; if you write long enough, you will write the truth about them. And they don't want to be exposed or the family skeletons dragged into the light.

But writers must write. They must write about alcoholism and abuse. They must write about adoption or racism or neglect. Writers have to tell their stories somehow. True, our stories can be disguised as fiction. But good writing is about conflict and struggle. And, ultimately, a lot of the pain of fiction comes from real life. And we have the right to tell the truth about what we've lived.

This probably will not make your mother happy. She might recognize herself in your aging character who routinely lies about her age. This character, Sheila (your mother's name is Shirley), is obsessed with looking young and spends lots of time and money on facelifts, tummy tucks, health spas. Sheila can't even remember her real hair color. Your mother, a redhead at sixty-three, is clearly hurt. She even threatens to disinherit you. Write anyway.

Maybe your sister resents the overweight, over-bearing, acne-scarred antagonist in your novel. Maybe she's been on a diet since seventh grade and has always claimed that her massive thighs and enormous behind stem from a glandular problem. However, your character is fat because she hides from life, spending her Saturday nights with jumbo bags of corn chips and candy bars, afraid of relationships and rejection. Your sister can't believe you'd put a fat person in your book. She accuses you of being an insensitive clod. Write about fat people anyway.

True, this is the only family you have. But also this is the only chance you have to write your truths, tell your story, live your dream. No matter what your family says, you know if you are a writer. Writers burn with the necessity to share their words. Writers must spin their tales and fantasies far out into the planet for others to discover. And finally, the farther these words travel, the more readers respond to us, the

greater our satisfaction. Tell your family that you love them and acknowledge their concerns, but don't let them stop you. Don't wait for your mother to die, your sister to lose weight, your brother to move out of the basement. Write the truth, and don't ask permission.

try this

Complete a story or essay that begins: My family never talks about the time _____

Basics

"The beginning of human knowledge is through the senses, and the fiction writer begins where human perception begins. He appeals through the senses, and you cannot appeal through the senses with abstractions."

FLANNERY O'CONNOR

Over the years I've come up with a simple list of characteristics to describe good writing. Each semester I drill this list into my students every chance I get, citing some well-known authorities. William Zinsser's book, *On Writing Well,* claims that few of us know how badly we write. This is, of course, bad news. But then Zinsser offers hope and guidance. He masterfully explains how simple, concise writing is the best writing. He warns that we must use no unnecessary words. Ever. It's the best writing advice there is.

Thus, good writing is concise.

Good writing is also clear. It should never leave the reader confused nor needing to reread your sentences to unlock some meaning that he or she can't grasp.

Good writing is vivid. It paints pictures in bold, dynamic strokes until the reader is lost in the seamless world of your words. Vivid writing makes readers "see" as if they're watching a movie inside their heads instead of black words on a white page. Vivid means bigger than life, bold, colorful, dynamic.

Good writing is lively. Each sentence flows to the next in a lively rhythm that the reader never wants to end. The sentences don't plod, drag, or get entangled. They march crisply along the page, and the reader is caught up and forced to turn page after page as your words unfold.

Good writing relies on strong, precise nouns and verbs. We strive to find the perfect word to describe each action, person, event, place, and thing.

Good writing hinges on a careful use of qualifiers, adjectives, and adverbs. Let your nouns and verbs do the work. Don't load your sentences with extras, or they'll look like gingerbread trim on a ranch-style home. Silly. Wasteful. My students sometimes heap four, five, six adjectives in a sentence, and when I point out this disgraceful excess, they're often shocked and offended. Beginning writers love adjectives. They squander adjectives like a gambler throwing away his winnings.

My journalism teacher once gave us an "F" every time we used the word "very." It was an effective reminder of how wimpy words like "very" are. Don't tell us your hero is very strong; instead describe him as strapping, Herculean, unbending, unequivocal, resolute.

As I edit my second drafts, I rid the copy of qualifiers: sort of, a bit, a little, too, rather, kind of, pretty much, quite, and very. They are a sure sign of a lazy writer. Qualifiers are timid and unconvincing. Get rid of them.

Good writing is conversational. Write like you talk, not how you wish you could talk. Or how your favorite college professor talked. Don't write to impress your readers; write to be understood. Forget jargon, multi-syllabic words, baby talk, tricks, and excess slang.

Good writing is sensory. Whether we describe our home town or a holiday dinner, our descriptions should ring with images for all the senses. We smell the spices in the pumpkin pie, the ocean air, the dog kennel. We hear the bird calls, the woman sighing, the hum of freeway traffic. We draw characters and scenes with enough detail so that the reader experiences them through all the senses. We describe the heat of the summer so precisely that the reader can feel its oppressive, sultry air that stifles ambition but ignites hatreds.

Good writing is full of specific details. We don't populate our stories with generic, fill-in-the-blank characters, but instead populate our prose with down-and-out cowboys, peep-show operators, shy secretaries, bashful four year olds, white-haired matrons, pimply teenagers, greedy bankers. At first glance, this character list might not look original. However, if you find the small, telling details—the limps, lisps, tattoos, bad hairdos, fake beauty marks, cheap underwear, wild eyebrows, and weird gestures that make them seem real—they will come to life.

Now, I'm not telling you to merely add adjectives to your writing. I'm suggesting that you hone in on details and specifics, bringing the reader close. Good writing is intimate. Is the sofa made of velvet, leather, Naugahyde? What kind of books are in the suspect's bookcase? What time of day is it? What does the air smell like? Is the detective's desk orderly or brimming with Dunkin' Donuts crumbs, an overflowing ashtray, Post-it Notes, incomplete forms, a toxicology report, files, message slips, and burger wrappers? Details characterize, provide a sneaky way to slip in insights. Don't write that there was a bowl of fruit on the table. Tell us there was a wooden bowl brimming with nectarines, Granny Smith apples, kumquats, bananas. Paint the picture. No faded black-and-white snapshots, please. We want color prints, close-ups, revealing, inspiring details.

You've heard it again and again; show, don't tell. We *show* our readers when we use solid nouns and verbs and specific details to bring our stories to life. We don't stand back from the action; instead we pan the camera into the midst of the scene and reveal the drama. Don't tell us the dog was mean; show us the dog snapping and sniveling at the mailman when he attempts to open the gate. Don't tell us the mailman was scared. Show him leaping backward, startled, dropping his mailbag and scattering envelopes on the sidewalk while he struggles to grab his mace.

Good writing avoids clichés. Clichés are another sign of laziness. Use clichés only when writing dialogue; avoid them like the plague in your writing. You see how easy it was to slip in a cliché—it rolls off our fingers like water off a duck's back. I've never seen water on a duck's back, so why would I choose a cliché to illustrate ease? A cliché is easy to spot because it's been said before and said too often. It's not new, it's not fresh, it's not interesting. However, sometimes clichés are sneaky—they show up in chiseled features, postcard pretty scenes, and piercing eyes. Beware.

Good writing is done in the active voice and the present tense whenever possible. The active voice and present tense pull the reader in and dispel confusion. Editors are fanatically aware of how easy it is to transform a manuscript by getting rid of the passive voice. In the original version, every sentence plods along, slow as a casket borne to a grave site. The passive voice hurts the eyes after a while. Don't inflict this pain on your readers.

Example of passive voice: The class was taught by me.

Example of active voice: I taught the class.

try this

Whenever possible, eliminate **qualifiers** and **intensifiers**. Good writing is distinct, accurate, and assured. Qualifiers and intensifiers make the writer appear uncertain and unsure.

Intensifiers: very, quite, absolutely, truly, completely, basically, absolutely, really, extremely, totally, so, perfectly, actually.

Example: Instead of completely surprised, astounded. Instead of very tired, exhausted.

Qualifiers: a little, sort of, kind of, rather, quite, very, pretty much, a bit, too.

Example: Instead of rather important, vital. Instead of sort of weak, limp.

Write Tight

Your first draft is important; it contains the passion of your ideas. But editing and rewriting, vital skills for every writer, make the writing fluid, yet concise. Good writers are good editors. Most of us need to rewrite our drafts three or four times before they are the polished gems that editors want to buy. While we edit, it's necessary to keep a few principles in mind. Editing generally isn't about adding words; it's pruning unnecessary words and scrutinizing style. As you edit your final drafts, consider these principles:

There should be no unnecessary words, thoughts, or paragraphs. Imagine that your manuscript is a movie set. Is there a purpose for all the actors on the set, or are some of them milling around, taking up space, crowding out the stars? Is the set jammed with furniture and so many knickknacks that we're distracted? Adjectives and adverbs are often decorative rather than necessary. Delete them. Write tight.

Whenever possible, write in the active voice. Take a long look at your prose and prune the passive verbs. Search out passive linking verbs: IS, AM, WAS, BE, BEEN, ARE, HAS, HAVE, HAD, MAY, CAN, MUST, MIGHT, WOULD, COULD, SHOULD, SHALL, WILL, DO, and replace them with active verbs whenever possible. While linking verbs are often necessary in our sentences, they slow down our writing if we rely on them. Use them sparingly. Active verbs are vigorous, pushing sentences along with bulldozer force.

Good writing is clean, precise, concise, and vivid.

Good writing starts out with a clash of cymbals, an intriguing puzzle or a fresh approach that hooks the reader, forcing him or her to read further. It's like walking past a bakery; the smell of chocolate and yeast envelopes us, and, before we know it, we've strolled inside and soon we're munching on a glazed doughnut. Good writing is irresistible.

How do you captivate readers? First, make sure that your words are about people. Inserting people into your openings applies to both fiction and nonfiction writing. Beginning writers often forget to put people in their opening scenes. They meander into the piece, establishing setting and tone and atmosphere. About six paragraphs later, after the reader is nodding off, they introduce a character. Bring the humans into your story from the start. Good beginnings startle, intrigue, pull us in. This doesn't happen unless we have people to care about.

Good writing introduces conflict in the opening paragraphs. This doesn't mean that a motorcycle has to crash into the hero, pinning his legs against a semitruck and rendering him crippled for life. It doesn't mean that the husband abandons his pregnant wife in the first line. But the writer must set up, at the very least, a sense of unease, foreboding, intrigue. Plant hints of the upcoming conflict. Make the husband turn away from the pregnant wife when she bends to plant a morning kiss. That grabs the reader's attention. They'll wonder what's wrong. Isn't he happy with the pregnancy? Is this baby planned?

Good writers sprinkle their writing with details. Don't confuse your readers or let them wallow in a muck of vague words. Draw a clear, clean picture. Details eliminate doubts. Readers know exactly what you're trying to say. Details are sensory. Readers smell the chicken soup bubbling on the stove, hear the faint hiss of the gas burner and the shuffling steps of the tired woman setting the table with mismatched blue bowls and jelly jars. Readers sense her despair from the slump of her shoulders and the worn bathrobe that she still wears at dinnertime. Details pull us in and bring the words to life.

Finally, when you've completed your final draft, read it out loud. The ears catch the bumps and inconsistencies that the eyes miss. Does it sound smooth, flowing, poetic?

try this

Write a story using five hundred words or less. Have you included conflict, details and dialogue?

EXAMPLE: Tight writing.

Time
by Ron Winn

The letter, address handwritten, was on the table when I got home. Return address somewhere in Ohio.

Hey, soldier, listen up . . .

Roy! Oh my gosh, Roy. Memories burst like fireworks. Boot camp, infantry training, jungle survival, Hong Kong R & R.

Hope this reaches you, buddy. Been a long time I know, but what's a little time between friends?

No time at all, soldier. Fifteen, eighteen years? Buddies forever.

I needed to write, man. Things are tough right now, and you were the somebody I could talk to when I needed things cleared up. Remember when Wiz got it? And when Petey lost his leg and shipped home?

I remember. Wiz—Wizchevski the Pole from Chicago—bled his life away into the jungle floor and Petey's leg disappeared in a flash of light and blood. Roy and I were there. Roy sat with Wiz for two days, watching him go. I sat with Roy for three days while he cried.

Remember Patti?

Patti! Roy's girl through high school. Perfumed letters, mini-mini skirts, "These Boots are Made for Walkin' . . ." I was best man at their wedding. Our last great time together.

Cancer took her, buddy. Last week. I sat with her and watched her go, a little bit at a time. You always seemed to know what to say. Even if you can't now, it helps me to know I was able to tell you. I've got family all around, but you're the one I have to tell to be able to let her go, to just let it be real. Like with Wiz.

I sit and hold the letter to my chest, holding Roy's head one more time, feeling him shake as he cries.

He's right. There is no time between then and now. Not for friends.

Write About Your Passions

Beginning writers should write about subjects they care about. When you write close to the heart, the writing has significance and substance.

Consider the classics written by Homer, Shakespeare, Tolstoy, Chekhov. These stories transcend time and geography because the authors wrote about universal themes that they held deep opinions about. Classics, although difficult to define, contain common themes that ring with the truth of human experience: betrayal, tragedy, lust, death, redemption, knowledge, love. These universal themes resonate because they're the glue of human existence. After all, we all hurt, we all try and fail, fall out of love, and make bad choices.

There are people who are born to save the world, who care deeply about whales, the rain forest, the ancient forest, and the homeless. The world needs humanitarians, activists, and someone to write about their issues. If you care deeply about the disappearing salmon, whales, dolphins, write about it.

Some of never us get over our stupid mistakes and childhood traumas. There are plenty of folks walking around who flush with shame when they remember their wet dreams or the time they got drunk and flirted with their married boss at the office Christmas party.

For writers, pain equals possibility. Recall how your first love dumped you for your best friend, the time your underwear slipped off in public, the first act when you forgot your lines. What were your emotions that day? How can you describe elation, sorrow, longing? Tell us about your physical reactions. Describe how your eyes misted, your hands shook, face flushed, heart pounded, ears rang, legs wobbled.

Recall when you or someone close to you were wrongly accused. Maybe the charge was cheating on a test or petty theft. You couldn't convince your accusers of your innocence. Summon your anger, frustration, conviction.

Now write an essay examining one of these issues or assign these passions to your fictional characters. Insert dramatic anecdotes into your nonfiction to expose the dilemmas within an issue. Breathe life into your words based on your beliefs, your passions, your hurts.

For example, say you're writing a story about a woman who is newly widowed. You've never been married, but your beloved collie was killed by a car when you were fourteen and you cried yourself to sleep for days. And when your grandmother died, you were too distressed to attend her funeral. You've always regretted not saying a final good-bye to your grandmother because in her eyes you shone like a night sky spilling over with diamond bright stars. Bid farewell to your grandmother through the words of your character mourning her husband.

Have you always felt strongly about racism or conservative politics? Do you think our political system is hopelessly corrupt? Do you think men or women are doomed to loneliness? That sexism is the root of all evil? Are you convinced that friendship is fraught with betrayal, that men are naturally unfaithful, that teenagers are psychopathic? Do you hate Republicans? Bigots? Evangelists? Wife batterers?

Do you love Christmas? Are you healed and joyous in nature? In church? In the arms of your lover? Does the world need more volunteers, recycling centers, teachers? Are you an ardent gardener, jogger, coin collector, wine connoisseur, gourmet cook, bird watcher?

Write about what you love and hate. There is too much apathy in our culture. Write with passion and your readers will respond.

try this

Write an essay about love, lust, greed, fear, envy, or another strong emotion. Dramatize your subject with details, but never directly use the word (emotion) that you're describing.

Read Critically

"Reading is to the mind what exercise is to the body."

RICHARD STEELE

Writers must be omnivorous readers. Read everything, but read critically. Good writers are alert, careful readers. As you read, examine the writer's techniques, tricks, style. I introduce Barbara Kingsolver to my students because her books illustrate solid style. Kingsolver, author of *Animal Dreams, The Bean Trees, Pigs in Heaven,* and *High Tide in Tucson* deserves the success she's generated from these amazing books.

One of Kingsolver's writing strengths is her gift for characterization. Her characters are carefully, yet imaginatively drawn. They're believable and engaging, yet quirky and rare. As readers, we find ourselves rooting for her characters, worrying about them, remembering them years after we were introduced.

Kingsolver also lovingly fleshes out her minor and secondary characters. In *The Bean Trees,* she describes her supporting character Lou Ann, a devoted reader of tabloid magazines, a professional worrier, who imagines that disaster lurks everywhere. Lou Ann believes that the only safe way to eat potato salad is by standing with your head inside the refrigerator. Kingsolver didn't just tell us that Lou Ann fears salmonella poisoning, she shows us. And makes us laugh.

Another of Kingsolver's strengths are her plots, tight and polished gems. Each scene adds to plot and character development; they don't exist extraneously. She begins *The Bean Trees* by describing a bizarre scene that colors the entire novel: Newt Harbine's father is blown high into the air by a tire he's inflating. The reader is immediately alerted that the narrator is uneducated, and her world, a small town in Kentucky, is a weird, backward place.

Early on, we're rooting for Taylor, the protagonist, hoping she escapes. After Taylor witnesses the tire explosion in the opening scene, she develops a tire phobia, a rare quirk, but believable in the hands of a skillful storyteller like Kingsolver.

A critical reading of Kingsolver's books also reveals that she's the reigning queen of metaphor. Metaphoric writing adds richness and lush layers of meaning and nuance to our stories. Her metaphors are lively comparisons, brilliant stretches between words and images. These arresting contrasts linger with readers for years. For example, she compares the teenage girls in Taylor's high school becoming pregnant and leaving school to seeds dropping off a poppyseed bun. Lou Ann gets a job packing salsa at the Red Hot Mama's salsa factory. Working conditions are hard, and the workers are often burned from the chilies they pack. Kingsolver writes that on days that they process extra-hot salsa, it slops onto the floor and their ankles burn as if they're standing on red ant hills.

Another Kingsolver talent is her ability to discuss complex issues without preaching. Taylor, bold and brash, moves to Arizona and blunders into situations that challenge her limited experience. As she grows, issues are exposed: sexism, racism, child abuse, the sanctity movement for illegal aliens. By the last sentence of *The Bean Trees,* readers are aware of Kingsolver's politics but aren't exhausted by them. It's a gentle kind of moralizing.

Readers are pulled into the plot and the issues through Taylor's unique perspective, her dilemmas, and finally her strengths. As we laugh and empathize with the cast of *The Bean Trees,* we're educated and ultimately delighted.

Don't just read, read critically. Observe the author's techniques, successes, and failures. When writers read, they make it an active experience.

try this

Return to one of your favorite books and read it as a writer. Underline effective passages and highlight sensory details. Note sparkling dialogue, brilliant characterization, resonating themes. What can other writers teach you?

Inspiration Is Everywhere

"When you're writing, you're trying to find out something which you don't know. The whole language of writing for me is finding out what you don't want to know, what you don't want to find out. But something forces you to anyway."

JAMES BALDWIN

A few years ago, I was walking in downtown Portland when I spotted a woman leaving a parking lot. Like most urban areas, Portland is populated with a mix of people; the homeless, the hip, office workers, students, and street kids. The woman I spotted belonged to none of these groups.

Instead, she appeared straight from the small towns of my Wisconsin childhood. She was overweight, lumpy, and awkward. She wore the same glasses and hair style that were popular in the late fifties. Her arms were covered with pimples, her face with acne scars, her purse was cheap plastic, her purple pedal pushers and sleeveless blouse strained at their polyester seams.

I couldn't stop myself. I followed her for blocks until she disappeared into an office building.

Later, I pulled out my notebook and sketched a quick description of the woman. But I couldn't forget her. A few days later she found her way into the novel I was writing and became a central character who shaped the plot.

Inspiration is everywhere.

I was walking in my neighborhood yesterday morning. I live in a neighborhood of quiet streets, landscaped yards, and gracious homes. Two teenagers walked across the street, then stopped for a long hug. The girl was sobbing, and her friend was murmuring comfort. I could hear her wet words, "I'm filthy. I'm a wreck. I smell like shit," she wailed. They resumed their walk. I wanted to follow but this time curbed my desire. Instead, I tried imagining the girl's problems. Had she run away from home? Was she attacked by someone? Had she been out all night drinking? I filed the image away. I haven't figured out what I'll do with this vignette, but a short story about a street kid is slowly shaping in the back of my mind.

It's not enough to notice everything and write it down. We must take the next step and ask questions. We must have empathy with those we meet. What makes our neighbor sad? What are her secrets, her fantasies? After I followed the woman through the downtown streets, I was full of questions. What would it be like to look like her? What did she see when she looked in the mirror? Where was she going? Who was her family? Where did she come from? What did she do for a living? Was she married or single? Yesterday I had more questions. What happened to the girl on the street? How did she get dirty? What do I remember about my Aunt Martha and the rest of the women from my childhood? What of this sadness, this longing to talk with them one more time, to go back in time and meet my ancestors?

Pay attention to your world, then let the images filter in and stir up questions. How can you respond to what's out there? Are you afraid? Intrigued? Delighted?

try this

Write a story, poem, or essay inspired by a walk through your neighborhood. How does it differ from a neighborhood in Newark or Memphis? How does it differ from where you grew up?

Suffering

"I work continuously within the shadow of failure."

GAIL GODWIN

William Styron, author of *Sophie's Choice* and *Confessions of Nat Turner*, writes at a tedious pace. His daily eight to ten hours of writing nets him only one finished page. He laments that writing is so painful he feels like appending a suicide note to the end of each page.

Writers must be realists, and every writer should expect to suffer. Sometimes the going gets rough. There will be days when you'd rather be sitting under a dentist's drill than at your computer. The advice remains the same: write anyway.

Suffering writers are everywhere. Writers suffer in Prague, in Provence, in Palo Alto. Face it, some days being a writer sucks. You'll have days of doubts and silence. At times you'll feel so scared and stalled that your head will throb, your eyes will burn, your shoulders will knot. Write anyway.

Writing is one of the few professions where people entertain thoughts of giving up when the going gets rough. Athletes play despite pulled tendons and broken bones. In the theater the adage is "the show must go on" despite attacks of nerves or illness. I've known musicians who practiced until they developed painful blisters on their fingertips. Eventually the blisters became calluses. They kept playing.

Expect some rain to fall, but learn to remain optimistic during times that defy a sunny outlook. Anyone who spends hours alone, involved in an artistic pursuit, lives in danger of dark moods and self-pity. These moods are inherent parts of spending time devoted to a creative process. In the midst of our work, we doubt, we question. It is part of the process, BUT it is usually temporary.

Suffering for writers comes in many forms. Sometimes it takes the form of insomnia. Insomnia is another symptom of fear. The clock ticks away precious hours and minutes; we toss, restless, haunted, exhausted. If only we could sleep.

Then there are the times when we can't pay our rent or buy our mother a birthday present because we've made financial sacrifices for our writing.

Writers sometimes suffer from the stuck-in-the-middle-of-the-novel-how-the-hell-am-I-going-to-end-this-thing misery.

There's suffering that's really another name for self-doubt; nobody will buy my work, so why bother writing?

Then there's the if-I-don't-get-out-of-this-place-and-talk-to-somebody-I'm-going-to-go-mad suffering. Otherwise known as loneliness.

Doubts. Debts. Fear. Fatigue. Loneliness. This is not a pretty scenario I'm painting. When we were in kindergarten and imagined our grown-up lives, suffering didn't enter into the picture. A nice house and a big dog and lots of chocolate cake and ice cream were our dreams. We probably planned to be a scientist, teacher, fireman. We didn't bargain for all this other stuff that goes with the writing life. This hurts.

Are there any answers to the suffering? Is it really intrinsic to the life style? Yes and no. As with all struggles, first admit your pain, then step back from the self-pity, the worrying and wallowing. Stop whining and start problem-solving.

Borrow some money or work a temporary job for a week or two when your funds get so low you can't afford the basics. Then come home each night and write. Write a long letter to your mother on her birthday and recall your favorite memories of her.

If your novel is stalled, find a way to get unstuck; talk with your characters, outline your plot, read other writers in your genre for inspiration. You're not the first writer to bog down in the deadly middle of a plot, nor will you be the last. Go back to basics. What motivates your characters? What do they stand for? Is the conflict compelling or gimmicky?

When the why-am-I-a-writer doubts persist, take action. Research a magazine that you've been wanting to write for, and send for its writer's guidelines. Visit bookstores or libraries and remember that every editor is in the business of buying writing. Editors and publishers need us. We are not parasites or supplicants or lowly life forms. But each writer must learn to be a marketer. If you're not good at selling your work, develop a relationship with somebody who is.

When you're going mad from being stuck at your computer, get away for a while. Go for a walk, pet the cat, make a phone call, invite friends for dinner. When the loneliness gets unbearable, find somebody to talk to; don't let it swallow you. Writing isn't about doing penance; weave enjoyment and rewards into your daily routine.

Here is what you shouldn't do when suffering overwhelms you: get drunk, kick your dog, yell at your children, burn your manuscript, blame your childhood, criticize your wife, consider suicide, quit, blame editors or publishers for your problems, give in to your fears that you're not good enough.

Go to your diary or your journal. Expose your pain, your doubts. Work with the darkness; don't give in to it. And remember that for most of us, the more we write, the less we suffer. If you adhere to the suggestions in this book, if you plunge yourself in the writing life, acknowledging your fears, yet not stopping because of them, your suffering **will** diminish. I'm convinced that if you open yourself to your creativity and believe in its infinite source, you will write often and easily. Using these suggestions, suffering slows, then becomes unnecessary, even stupid.

try this

Write an imaginary correspondence between two people. Decide on the nature of their relationship. Your letter writers could be lovers, a grandparent and his or her grandchild, a prison inmate and his or her pen pal, or childhood friends separated by thousands of miles.

Suffering Is Optional

"There are times when words come, and they have a palpability to them. I hate to use this word but they really do have a vibration. When they come out of my body, they come out with a certain hum or sound. That hum or sound has meaning attached to it—not because the words connote something, but because they are something in and of themselves. At the same time, they feel like myself. It's as if I am touching this being that I don't get to hold in my hands otherwise. Maybe that's why writers often like to write at dawn or late at night when things are very quiet; there's something magical about those times. Magical about the light. Magical about the stillness. We look for a pristine setting in which we can encounter ourselves. Of course, as I was saying this, I was thinking about all the writers I know who like to write at cafes and in New York and on the subway. That's a whole other scene, but there is some way in which one comes alive, enacting oneself in that open moment."

DEENA METZGER

———————————

One of my favorite Buddhist sayings is that while life is difficult, suffering is optional. Most of us suffer because we choose to. We're miserable because we don't have the strength to stop wallowing, whining, and acting out our victim role. And admit it, suffering is rather romantic.

And then there are days that, despite your best intentions, you sag, you falter, you think you're losing your mind. There are days when I'd rather volunteer for medical experiments than make my living as a writer. It's too hard and lonely. There's not enough money or satisfaction. But there's another side to this issue, a larger truth.

Last summer a young man enrolled in my writing workshop. He'd long entertained notions of writing but, like so many of us, buried his dreams and was working in a mustard bottling plant. The pieces that he wrote in class were marvels of poetic imagery, thoughtful analysis, startling imagination. He was fabulous.

In about the middle of the semester, however, he raised his hand and asked with complete seriousness, "Aren't all writers crazy?" I was stunned at his sincerity. So we spent some time looking at the ugly myths about writers and how they are supposedly addicted, twisted, miserable, self-absorbed, masochistic.

Forget about all the suicidal, self-destructive, alcoholic, psychotic writers whom you've heard about. Chances are that these folks might have been messed up if they'd chosen to be podiatrists. Being a writer doesn't mean you're destined to be wretched. Of course, there are days when the work doesn't satisfy. Sure there are days when the words won't come out right. Frustrating, long, maddening, rotten times.

But bankers have bad days. Wall Street brokers have lots of tough times. Teachers suffer doubts and despairs. So how come writers get such a bad rap? Why are we the crazies among the professions? Because it's romantic. Because the arts aren't supported much in this country, and our younger generations aren't writing books, they're writing ad copy. Because if we keep spreading the lies that artists are whacko, young people won't go into the arts, they'll stay in line, working in the hive-like cubicles and droning vapidness of corporate America.

Because many great writers were more than a little twisted: Williams, Faulkner, Plath, Hemingway, Capote. But don't buy into their examples. Writing might have exacerbated their problems, but don't blame writing for making these folks crazy or alcoholic, they probably were destined for trouble no matter what they did for a living. And remember, there a lot of writers who don't cheat on their wives or stick their heads in the oven. They drive mini-vans and coach soccer, attend PTA, invest in IRAs, are nice to their mothers, and go to church. Judge each writer individually, not as a group.

Statistics prove that dentists suffer from high levels of depression and suicidal thoughts because their patients are afraid of them. It seems that people just can't warm up to doctors who thrust sharp objects into their mouths and drill holes in their teeth. As far as I know, these statistics haven't lowered dental school admissions. Causing your patients pain is part of the bargain in dentistry. I know several dentists who are obscenely happy with their profession. They didn't fall for the stereotype. And their patients like them even when their mouths ache.

Another warning: Most suffering that comes with writing comes from feeling blocked. Once you work through your fears and write regularly, blocks just don't happen as often. Like me, there will come a day when each time you sit at your computer, the words will pour out. Most days I can hardly type fast enough to get my thoughts down. I'm a vessel, a conduit from a creative well-spring. The more I write, the happier I am.

Over the years, I've watched my students become transformed through their writing, so I know it can happen to you, too. On the first day of class they grumble and complain about how blocked and frustrated they are. But by the last class in the semester, they're changed. A lot of them glow. They're confident, excited. They're forming writers' groups. They're turned on and hopeful. They've tapped into a source, their creativity, and it's rich and deeper than oceans, and available to all of us.

try this

Those of us who write are taking a journey of deep self-knowing. Many of us don't have a choice; writing seems interwoven into our destiny like our families or the color of our skin. Accept your path gratefully. Write about why you love to write. Count all the good stuff: the ease, the flow, the recognition, the unfolding, and joy that only comes with writing.

Poverty

No worst, there is none. Pitched past pitch of grief,
More pangs will, schooled at forepangs, wilder wring.
Comforter, where, where is your comforting?

GERARD MANLEY HOPKINS

Forget about John Grisham's latest multi-million dollar publishing deal or the undeserved phenomenon of lousy books like *Bridges of Madison County*. If you're only writing for fame and fortune, you're writing for the wrong reasons.

A struggling writer once asked a famous editor for his best advice. The editor replied, "Get used to poverty." This probably doesn't comfort most of you, but let's consider the editor's words. Writing isn't only about money; writing is about following a sacred calling the way that young men are called to the priesthood. The humblest novitiate among us must first possess a sincere desire to write. Desire is a powerful notion. Desire propels us past our fear of poverty and keeps us writing.

When you first start writing, you will probably not make any money. This is the dismal reality of the writing business. You might be the exception, but most beginners should understand that writing requires an unpaid apprenticeship.

As I see it, there are two ways to make it as a writer. Let's go back to John Grisham. He wrote his first books while employed full-time as a lawyer and a legislative aide, working sixty to seventy hours a week. But he set himself a goal to write one legal pad page each day. He persisted, wrote the first novel, which was repeatedly rejected, and went on to write the second, still maintaining his schedule and writing goals. Grisham proves that working a full-time job while writing a first novel is possible. He believes that the key is to establish specific goals and adhere to them.

The second approach to writing is more risky and, frankly, the one that I prefer. Some of us choose not to work full-time while we get serious about writing and instead pare down our lives so that writing can take precedence. We choose a job that pays the basics but allows a regular block of writing hours. The job shouldn't be too challenging or time consuming. Pizza delivery, waiting tables, carpentry, bartending, security guard, house painting are all good career choices for writers.

This approach might involve a temporary vow of poverty. Forget about European vacations, designer clothes, champagne. Find a cheap place to live, learn how to concoct large batches of stick-to-the-ribs soup, keep an older car running, and buy everything from toilet paper to clothes on sale. If you love to write, this life can be rich and rewarding.

There are alot of success stories in the publishing world. Sometimes the publishing world rocks with the news of six-figure advances, movie deals, and instant critical acclaim for a beginning writer. These jackpot, rainbow-end stories don't happen often. And don't forget: that if you scratch the surface of most overnight successes, you'll probably find a writer who's spent years learning his craft before he was discovered. Like John Grisham.

If you are reading this book, you have the opportunity to earn a decent income as a writer. Some day. After hundreds of dues-paying hours at a computer. Some of you will earn only enough money for postage and paper. There are no guarantees in this profession.

Do What You Love, The Money Will Follow by psychologist Marsha Sinetar was one of the first books about discovering your appropriate livelihood. She says that work is a natural form of self-expression because we must devote so much of our life to it. Sinetar outlines the satisfaction, self-esteem, and self-knowledge that comes from doing the work that makes us happy, as opposed to going to work merely to pay the bills.

We write because it is our first love, and we make sacrifices, including risking poverty, to pursue our art. We hope wealth follows eventually, but the underlying belief is that the writing life is one of integrity. Conversely, writers can be among the richest people on the planet. One definition of prosperity is living happily and contentedly no matter what our assets.

You must write because you must write. When you don't write, you become dejected and empty and pallid. We don't choose writing for fame and fortune; writing chooses us. I would rather write than be a rock star, scientist, symphony conductor, heart surgeon, actress, movie director, business mogul. Writing is as much a part of me as the blood that runs in my veins. Writing is intoxicating, stimulating. Writing comes between me and the darkness that lies all around. Writing is my heart. And that, my friends, is wealth.

try this

We need to remember that even the greatest writers started at the same place—as unknown beginners. Research the lives of your favorite writers. How old were they when they started writing? When did they first get published? Did they have a mentor? What is their daily writing routine? Do they have advice for beginning writers?

Inner Qualities

"We are all apprentices in a craft where nobody becomes a master."

ERNEST HEMINGWAY

Writers must possess certain attributes to sustain them on the long road to publication.

If you have a deep rooted fear of poverty, forget about being a writer. It's a risky, long-term commitment. However, if you're naturally a risk taker, you're a candidate for the writing life. Writers are also resilient because they need to bounce back from rejection and criticism.

Writers are resourceful. Not only do they find silver linings in every rejection, they discover gold and emeralds in rain, mud, hormonal tides, the stuff of everyday life. Writers discover grace in mundane experiences because most of life provides the source of our work. Sometimes being resourceful means living on less money, and it could mean networking, searching diligently for the right agent or publisher.

Writers don't expect others to understand their drive, their passion to write.

Writers are optimists; they know they'll succeed despite doubts, lulls, and setbacks.

Writers see themselves as an unstoppable force like those old Charlie Brown cartoons in which a snowball starts rolling downhill, scooping up Snoopy, shovels, mittens, and half the kids in the neighborhood before its mammoth bulk hits the bottom of the hill.

Writers are patient.

Writers are motivated and committed.

Writers are active, involved, connected with their work and the writing community.

Writers trust their instincts and their abilities.

Writers are disciplined.

Writers have perspective, are able to stand back and see the big picture.

And finally, writers are frail. We don't like hurt, hard knocks, bad luck. We're lazy, weak, cowardly. We're human. Not goddesses, heroes, perfected beings. We haunt our friends with our whining and plot problems. Borrow money from our family. Beg strangers to read our work. We're self-absorbed and a little haughty because we're certain that our tribe, Writers, are quite superior to most other tribes.

Somewhere along the way, we learn that we can't avoid the struggles that are part of the writing process, but we can gracefully endure. We proceed with assurance and dignity. And, being human, we believe in our ability to improve, deepen, change. We learn that writing regularly makes us stronger.

These character traits are, of course, applicable to other professions. Devote yourself to your art. Your character will improve. People will whisper mostly good things behind your back. Success won't happen overnight, but it will happen.

try this

Study the lives of men and women whom you admire. What can you learn from how they lived their lives, pursued their goals? What traits carried them through difficult times? How are they different from you? How can you emulate their strengths?

Fantasies

"Light tomorrow with today."

ELIZABETH BARRETT BROWNING

———————————

Here's my favorite fantasy: I am seated in the audience at the Academy Awards in the not-too-distant-future, decked out in a red, strapless evening gown, my hair elegantly coifed, looking like I was born to mingle with the Hollywood crowd. The announcer bellows the winner of the best original screenplay: ME. I stumble to the dais, dazed with gratitude. I stutter a few sincere thank-yous and then get to the heart of my acceptance speech, reminding all the struggling artists of the world to persevere because if I can make it, there is hope for all writers.

Another favorite fantasy: I am a guest on *Oprah!*, or the *Today* show, or any nationally televised talk show, decked out in an elegant but professional red suit. I am interviewed by the show's host. The studio audience is enthralled, most of them clutching copies of my book, eager to beg for my autograph. The host confesses, teary-eyed, that my book has changed her life. Humbly, I acknowledge her gratitude and tell America how I came to write my best seller.

And so it goes. Fantasies are fun; fantasies are a great escape for days when writing is ten parts drudgery, one part inspiration. Find a fantasy. Play it on the screen in your head. Try it on for size. Can you see yourself there?

Our dreams are what keep us going. Especially if we write screenplays, fiction, and book-length projects. A novel can take years to write; it's a long way between the first glimmers of the plot and "the end." That means a lot of days spent alone in a room. That's where dreams come in handy. Go ahead, imagine your book-signing tours, guest appearances, prestigious awards, lunch with your agent at "21," whatever represents glamour and rewards. Most successful writers know that editing the final draft is tedious, book tours are exhausting, and personal appearances are a bore. Success means spending time alone in a hotel room, jet lag, negotiating contracts, bad-hair days when you want to look fabulous.

Hang on to your fantasy, but don't replace it with the real stuff: putting word after word after word on the page. Keep your fantasies for your low tides when you need a dream to push onward.

try this

In great detail, write a fantasy about your writing career. See yourself accepting the Pulitzer, getting published in the *New Yorker*, hopping the globe on a book-signing tour, meeting Jay Leno. Next, look at the message behind the fantasy. What are you striving for? Recognition? Financial security? Impact?

Writing Is A Job

"Writing is a craft. You have to take your apprenticeship in it like in anything else."

KATHERINE ANNE PORTER

More bad news. Writing is a job. And what's worse, it's not an easy job. If you want to be a professional writer, you need to understand that you're a business person who just happens to write. This isn't romantic. This is real.

What writing is not: it is not a hobby nor a cure for depression, a way to impress your mother, take revenge on your sister, embark on an ego trip, entertain a passing fancy until we establish our real careers, engage in cocktail party chic repartée, follow a quick road to fame, a way to get noticed.

Writing is a job. Like stocking groceries or fixing broken arms or growing apples or teaching mathematics. We train for it, and, if we persist, we will be paid for it. Probably not as much as for fixing arms but more than for stocking groceries or teaching math.

If it's a job, that means that we spend twenty, thirty, forty, fifty hours a week at our job. Not a few minutes here or there.

Writing is not for dabblers. It's for laborers. Men and women of the cloth. Believers. Toilers.

Write or shut up. There's no room for anything else.

try this

Write a job description for yourself. Describe all the aspects of writing, including editing, research, and marketing. How can you bring a new level of professionalism into your writing routine?

Simple Words Are Best

"Clutter is the disease of American writing. We are a society strangling in unnecessary words, circular constructions, pompous frills, and meaningless jargon. . . . Our national trait is to inflate and thereby sound important. The airline pilot who announces that he is presently anticipating experiencing considerable precipitation wouldn't dream of saying that it may rain. The sentence is too simple—there must be something wrong with it. But the secret of good writing is to strip every sentence to its cleanest components"

WILLIAM ZINNSER

When my daughter was young, I read her bedtime stories every night. Like most children, she had her favorite books that we read again and again. Twenty years later, I remember the sweet words to *Good Night Moon* or *Pat the Bunny* that lulled her to sleep. One of her favorite books was *Simple Pictures are Best*. This story was set about one hundred years ago when itinerant photographers traveled the countryside taking pictures of rural families.

The book opens with the photographer posing a farmer and his wife in front of their farm house. The couple is childless, but proud of their pets, livestock, and crops. They keep adding more of their prized possessions to the photo shoot: the cat, a flower pot, a cow, a chicken. With each addition the photographer, crouched behind his black cloth and tripod warns, "Simple pictures are best." After much commotion, the yard is crowded with all the relics of farm life, but there's a problem. The bull has become aroused by all the excitement. Snorting dangerously, he charges the scene. The last image that the photographer captures on film is the enraged bull's head. The photo bears out the photographer's warning: simple pictures are best.

Beginning writers are like that farm couple. They start with a simple concept and a few good, clean nouns and verbs, but they get carried away and weave in prepositional

phrases, qualifiers, adjectives, and adverbs. Words rarely mentioned in everyday conversation are sown into our sentences with drunken abandon. Beginning writers want to show off, to display their vocabulary and college education. Often they do this is by inserting long, multi-syllabic words. Or they toss in jargon or literary quotes and thick, convoluted descriptions and redundancies. The scenes drip with imminent danger and surreptitious liaisons. Weather is sinister, descriptions run to words like sheepish or girlish or garish. By the time the reader plows through these sentences, they have lost interest, missed the writer's meaning, and won't be lured back into the writer's messy prose.

Why? Because simple words are best. The English language is full of gems that convey meaning and do the work that needs to be done in our sentences. Our sentences don't need lots of words of Latin origin or nouns that have turned into verbs, like parenting or journaling.

Good writing incorporates lots of three, four, five, and six letter words of Anglo-Saxon origin. Words that you've known since you were small. Words like cow, sun, snow, star, moon, home. Words that convey their meaning and emotion in their sound like lull, swish, vex, jingle, mist, whirl, snag, beguile, slobber, smirk, flay, whiz, buss, swagger, dazzle, and daze. Words that are clean and simple and honest.

try this

Take a look at this word list and compare it with your latest composition. Are these the kind of words that form your sentences? Or are you showing off? Guess what? Nobody's impressed by your long words. Long, multi-syllabic words usually don't contain much emotion and they confuse most readers. Return to the words that resound and fill the page with classic beauty. Simple words are best: lean, blast, dip, hush, damp, dank, muck, slush, lush, purr, dim, lank, moon, star, stir, vex, dip, roar, stalk, stun, skip, bare, stark, bomb, rank, snow, stow, limp, stink, pound, steam, waste, stamp, swish, rip, skid, sway, grope, stump, daze, baby, deer, swarm, tide, whirl, scat, swipe, kin, bask, canoe, queer, stomp, swirl, steal, sack, swamp, camp, scream, slide, mourn.

Write a five to seven hundred word story or essay using words made up of six letters or less.

Write a five to seven hundred word story or essay using words made up of five letters or less.

EXAMPLE: Writing With Five-letter Words

THE PERMANENT SOLUTION
Sharon Wyda Collison

My Mom and Aunt Peg were the best of pals and the best of foes, some of the time all in one day. "Thick as thieves," Nana would say. Aunt Peg's kid, Rose, and me were best buds. Not one thing about us was alike. She was thin, I was a chunk. She was quiet. I was loud. She was a slob. I was neat. I was plain. She was fancy. Well, maybe one thing about us was alike. Our moms liked to drink.

Rose's hair was long. Black as blue. Wavy as the sea. My hair was light. Thin as a veil and had the look of a broom that stood on its straw, bent at an odd angle from years of use.

I don't know if I was ever at Rose's house. Aunt Peg and Rose were at ours all the time. They were there that day, too.

I sat in a chair. My feet not far from the floor. Aunt Peg pulls a perm box out of her purse and puts it on the table. My feet swung as Aunt Peg tore off the curls of the girl on the box.

On the table were three bottles: one pink, one clear, and one with 4 Roses on the label. My mom and Aunt Peg drank out of this one. Aunt Peg gave the cap a twist and said she saved fifty bucks. My mom's eyes didn't buy what they heard. Aunt Peg said she saved it out of Uncle John's pants. Said the perm was on her. It was a big laugh.

As the cap hit the table, sting hit my nose. Soon sting hit my eyes. My head. Sting went down my neck. Aunt Peg tried to roll my hair extra tight to get in that extra wave like the girl on the box. Aunt Peg put a clear cap on my head. My mom put rags in the cap and *Queen for a Day* on the TV. Rose and me went out in the yard. I saw my face in the glass of the door. Eyes slant like my China doll.

We could hear the lady cry her story on the TV. We could hear my mom and Aunt Peg cry with her. Soon we could only hear Aunt Peg. Rose didn't want to play hide-and-seek, just hide. They forgot the perm. Forgot me. Forgot sober. The sun dried the perm on my hair.

My mom's voice was a siren. It gave me a scare. So did the yank up the stairs. I held the rag tight above my eyes. My head under the spigot. My skin still red where the pink stuff came out.

They took out the pins, dried my hair, and began to poke, crimp, wet, brush, comb. There! I ran to my room. Could not wait to see. My eyes met the mirror. I shut the door. Hid in the coats. I knew I had to run away. It was the only way out. I put some stuff in a paper bag. I snuck past Mom and Aunt Peg's voices loud in the hall. Past Rose in back of the couch. I didn't get far. Too many looks. Too many stares. I hid under the porch. That's where I stayed. Long past the calls of my Mom. Past Rose's good-bye. Past the feet of my Aunt Peg as she drug Rose into the taxi.

My dad's work boots paced by the side of the porch. The sun went down and the bugs came out. I could smell the damp under the house mixed with the perm in my hair. I heard my belly. My head began to pound as I held back the cries. My nose ran and tears began to seep into my mouth. I could taste the salt. I felt the touch of my dad's hands as he tried to pull me out. They felt warm and safe. My dad held me close. He told me I was his best girl. My sobs only sighs in his arms.

Like wire in the hands of a bored child, I cut it off short. I liked it. It was a permanent solution.

Tools

"It is not wise to violate the rules until you know how to observe them."

T.S. ELIOT

———————————

Like a wound-up drill sergeant, I urge my students to pay attention to the nouns and verbs in their writing. I promise them that if they simply choose only specific nouns and active verbs, their writing will improve dramatically. And it works because as the semester progresses, their writing improves, becomes sleek and vibrant.

Use active verbs whenever you can. Verbs are the most important part of your sentences, the most useful of all the writer's tools. They propel your sentences, push the plot along. Active verbs are vivid, exciting, exact. Passive verbs are sluggish; the writing simpers and fizzles and lacks life.

Scrutinize your verbs ruthlessly. Are they perfect? Do they propel your ideas forward? When I edit other writers' books, the first style element I examine is the verbs. Usually I ruthlessly slash the passive verbs and exchange them for active ones. I trade dull, serviceable verbs for precise, exciting verbs. While these sound like small changes, my surgery transforms the books into noticeably better works.

Try it yourself. Replace ordinary verbs with more descriptive verbs. Instead of using ask, have your characters wheedle, coax, beg. Instead of walk, make your character sidle, skip, linger, dance. Collect verbs the way you'd collect baseball trading cards or Hummel figurines. Verbs are brisk winds blowing across billowing sails. Verbs are as necessary as a hammer to a carpenter, a scalpel to a surgeon. We wouldn't pound nails with a pair of scissors or slice into a body with a potato peeler. Use vivid verbs and you're using the right tool.

Vivid verbs don't need adverbs to explain them. Don't write, "He walked quickly," when you can say loped, sprinted, galloped. Adverbs usually are unnecessary and tacked on to bolster imprecise, wimpy verbs. The fewer adverbs you use, the better your writing becomes.

132

Beginning writers have problems with nouns because they don't search out the perfect nouns for each sentence. Instead, they jot down vague nouns, imagining that they'll suffice, then tack on an adjective to dress it up. We call a dwelling a little house instead of a cabin, hut, or hovel. We write tall building when we mean skyscraper; tree when we mean elm; headpiece when we mean tiara; jewelry when we mean bracelet. Precise nouns paint a vivid picture in the reader's head. Precise nouns are often sensory. Your readers can taste, smell, see, hear, feel, and sense your descriptions. They know exactly what you're trying to say. Precise nouns remove doubt.

try this

Here is a list of verbs that you can be proud of. Choose ten words at random and use them as the basis of a five hundred-word piece.

Glisten, simmer, blast, careen, stammer, squawk, gallop, wiggle, shriek, grope, zoom, gallop, bludgeon, pelt, glimmer, roast, bellow, badger, flinch, putter, zigzag, twinkle, shimmy, yak, simper, squint, whisk, gobble, thump, simmer, ram, gush, wedge, stew, stammer, hijack, sully, flutter, traipse, badger, simper, flog, twist, dally, squish, tromp, shirk, yammer, screech, saunter, tweak, cower, squeeze, growl, wobble, gorge, tickle, tiptoe, skewer, leap, sneak, sidle, swig, sear, toil, flicker, belch, blubber, bluff, nip, putter, stew, careen, sprint, puncture, plummet, baptize, banish, bombard, blurt, mash, gnaw, ooze, keen, needle, trample.

Write a five hundred-word piece based on ten nouns from the following list. Don't choose the words deliberately; select them in a random pattern: fireflies, pansy, doe, mosquito, tulip, shepherd, lover, mountain, smoke, veil, flashlight, collie, lace, trollop, silver, lilac, policeman, sofa, Satan, dragon, mule, dew, gangster, asphalt, detective, wheelchair, corset, handkerchief, rugby, toothpaste, ivy, orgasm, hammer, worm, crayon, dusk, troll, fern, stars, willow, vinegar, convict, fedora, blue jay, moon, ice cream, freeway, candlelight, monk, thunderstorm, houseboat, ballerina, pasta, cougar, raspberries, plow, lightening, zebra, troglodyte, warden, campaign, flash flood, cannibal, cowboy, catsup, spoon, slug, calico, tomato, beggar, zenith, orgy, bunting, pension, sodbuster, scaffold.

133

Show, Don't Tell

*"I do a lot of rewriting. It's very painful. You know it's finished when
you can't do anything more to it, though it's never exactly the way you want
it. . . . Most of the rewrite is cleaning. Don't describe it, show it. That's
what I try to teach all young writers—take it out! Don't describe a purple
sunset, make me see that it is purple. The hardest thing in the world is
simplicity. And the most fearful thing, too. You have to strip yourself of all
your disguises, some of which you didn't know you had. You want to write a
sentence as clean as a bone. That is the goal."*

JAMES BALDWIN

A few years ago when I started teaching children's writing classes, I went back to my childhood memories. I remembered how much fun it was to write about monsters and made-up creatures, how as a girl I adored every Disney movie. I designed a class based on these memories and my students write about ghosts, monsters, heroes, myths, witches, and little people.

While explaining "show, don't tell" to my young students, we discuss our nightmares. We list our physical reactions to bad dreams: pounding heart, rapid breathing, sweating, tingling, numbing fear, all explicit descriptions of our body waking in terror. Instead of vague descriptions or reactions, I urge my students to write about fear by remembering their own nightmares. Making the reader **experience** the story is tricky but not impossible. Take a long look at your passages, and whenever possible insert verbs that make the action compelling and alive.

Modern readers aren't patient. Exposed to fast-paced entertainment from television, videos, sound bites, they want a quick read. They're not willing to wade through long paragraphs of exposition or lengthy ramblings. Another issue, however, is that long descriptions don't inform; instead, they keep the reader out of the story, limit his or her involvement. Telling is summarizing, observing from afar, then reporting to the reader

what you (the writer) have observed. This keeps the reader removed from the text. Sometimes it's also lazy, sloppy, the easy way out.

Readers want to be involved, they want writing to **show.** If you show the readers what you're seeing, the writer and the readers are looking at the scene at the same time; the reader become immersed in the story. Showing is necessarily detailed, specific. The readers witness the action. Ultimately, the readers are satisfied because they sense that they are there, involved, engrossed in the scene. How is this done? The novice writer tells us (the readers) that the man is upset when he walks into the room. The experienced writer shows the man storm into the room, slam the door, bang his fist on a table and scream, "I hate that jerk!" He's clearly upset.

When we show in our writing, we use specific, active verbs, not adjectives or passive verbs. When my students ask me how to describe the backdrop, setting, or character without writing long paragraphs of exposition, I suggest that they imagine writing as if it were a strip tease. An experienced stripper doesn't simply shrug off her costume and call it a night. Instead, first she slips off her gloves, then peels off her stockings, slides off her garter belt; well, you get the picture. She teases her audience, piece by piece. Showing works best when we weave short examples throughout the text instead of inserting long blocks of description.

Short descriptions work better than long ones. Short bits also sound natural. Use the characters' thoughts, or small actions to reveal who they are. Don't invent long explanations in dialogue. In real life people don't tell each other what they already know, and in fiction this will sound artificial. Instead, summarize; give character background, motivation, and setting, scattering small pieces of exposition throughout the book or article. Showing through dialogue, inner thoughts, details, nuance, and anecdotes, creates scenes and characters that are believable and rich.

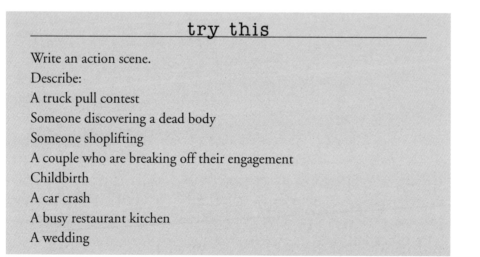

try this

Write an action scene.
Describe:
A truck pull contest
Someone discovering a dead body
Someone shoplifting
A couple who are breaking off their engagement
Childbirth
A car crash
A busy restaurant kitchen
A wedding

Remembering Childhood

"Ultimately, all this new college atmosphere wasn't enough to yank me from my roots. I carried my life in Farmingdale within me wherever I went. Personal power could not come from college or an English lit book. It had to come from deep within me. I had to go back and reclaim, transform what I had inherited at home. Eventually I had to stop running from what I had been given. If I opened to it, loneliness could become singleness; lethargy and boredom would transform into open space. Those fearful, negative feelings could become my teacher. . . . But if I wanted to survive—no, not just survive, I wanted glory, I wanted to learn how to grow a rose out of a cement parking lot—I had to digest the blandness and desolation of my childhood and make them mine. I couldn't run away, even though I tried, because in fact, my roots were all I had. . . . Writing became my vehicle for transformation, a way to travel out of that nowhere land. And because writing is no fool, it brought me right back in. There was no place else to go, but moving my hand across the page gave me a way to eat my landscape, rather than be eaten by it."

NATALIE GOLDBERG

---

136   Willa Cather said that our first fifteen years provide writers with the basic materials we work with for our whole lives.

Our early years are an endless source of riches. Childhood is a time like nothing else. As children we lived in a strange world, our small bodies caught in mysterious contradictions swirling around us, as we tried to learn the rules, have a little fun, and figure out grown-ups who often didn't make sense or explain things nearly enough. Because we were small, we were often overlooked or not taken seriously. Maybe we grew up in a home where we never allowed to talk back, have opinions, get angry. Or some of us got too much attention, were smothered and babied to death by parents who were terrified that some day we might leave them to their own emptiness. Many of us look back at our childhood and realize that some of the adults back then were inept at best, or just plain whacko. And some of us realize that we had a great time, that we were blessed.

When we become parents, we understand that most of us are clueless when it comes to raising kids, so we just muddle along the best we can, adlibbing as we go along, hoping that it will somehow work out and our children won't grow up to be terrorists. When we become parents a light shines on our past, and we start making peace with it. When we become writers we purposefully shine that high-watt lantern and take a good, hard look at how we got to be the way we are.

It doesn't matter if your whole family needed therapy or an intervention, or if things were so wonderful at your house that you made the Waltons look depraved. The important thing is to retrace the magic, to remember with a kid's wonder and awe. It's important to recall the *quality* of childhood, the way a summer day stretched with endless heat and promise. Remember how the future yawned so enormous that anything seemed possible. How the smallest things—winning a pair of goldfish at the county fair—were golden delights. The world was tall and grand and goofy.

In order to survive the weirdness of being small, children learn to pay attention. In fact, they pay close, careful attention to the sights and sounds around them. They're closer to the ground in more ways than one. They're tuned in to nuance and secrets because they don't have much power. The powerless among us have to be nimble, adaptable, ready to please. Take this awareness and look around at how big the world is.

Childhood memories have texture. Our early years are filled with ritual, holidays and routines that are linked to the senses. Go back. What do you smell? I remember how the flower beds edging our house held a fragrant sweep of lily-of-the-valley and the tiny glory of their little white bells. I remember how the honeysuckle that grew near the dining room bay window had a perfume so sweet and thick and sensuous.

Go back. What do you see? My grandfather's antique dresser was positioned under a slanted ceiling and held a mound of coppery pennies glinting, beckoning. To me, these coins represented unheard of wealth.

Go back. What did you touch? There were pink bleeding hearts in grandma's back yard and we gently peeled them apart to form elegant ballet slippers suitable for fairies.

Go back. What did you taste? I can still taste the too-sweet flavors of penny candy from the five-and-dime store—licorice whips, root beer barrels, candy corn, malted milk balls, circus peanuts.

Go back. What did you hear? My grandmother is rocking in her kitchen, humming nameless, made-up melodies and nonsense choruses, the chair squeaking against the old linoleum floor. "Twee, dee, dee, dah, too loo, rah, looh, rah," she sang.

And time passed, and I was no longer a child, but the younger me lives in all that I remember and write.

Go back and remember the smells of Thanksgiving at your grandmother's, the deep secrets of your mother's closet, finding your pastel Easter basket nestled behind the sofa. Remember the time you had the mumps, what you did on Saturday nights, your brother's friends, babysitters, and next-door neighbors.

The first assignment in most of my writing classes is to travel back to a memorable childhood event or holiday. As the students read these pieces out loud, we are all amazed at how many sensory details they remember. At how rich and honest and poignant the memories. I've heard heart-breaking stories in these classes: One man wrote about traveling alone by train when he was five, on his way to live with relatives whom he'd never met. This trip was scheduled after his mother was placed in an asylum. His relatives, strange Christian fundamentalists, called her Satan, and he never saw her again.

Yvon, a student who wants to write children's books, wrote about the time she had the measles and about her father's tender care, which included painting red spots on her doll. Her story was even more moving when we learned that her mother had run off with another man and their small farm community was rocked by this shocking event.

I've never forgotten another student's hilarious description of a family vacation. She piled into a Ford station wagon along with her brother, parents, and their sheepdog, and they drove from California to Canada, camping along the way. Her father, an alcoholic, drove with a bottle of Jim Beam conveniently parked between his legs and her mother, as usual, pretended that everything was normal. The detail, however, that made the whole class roar was her memory of how their sheepdog leaned over the backseat and drooled continuously on her and her brother. Her mother, apparently ever resourceful, draped towels over their heads, and so they rolled along thousands of miles, wearing towels.

My students have trotted out odd-ball and dysfunctional families, summer vacations spent at their grandparents' farms, Fourth of July picnics, Halloween parties, the terrors of the first day of school, brushes with death, ethnic feasts, and meals so disastrous and inedible that they deserve some ghastly prize.

Go back. No matter what your childhood was like, I guarantee that your early memories can deeply infuse your adult creativity. Let the kid you once were spark wonder for the often-weary, sometimes cynical adult.

I write about my childhood all the time. I was the troubled girl with freckles, scabby knees, and a pony tail riding a red Schwinn bicycle as fast as she could to escape home. I still remember a particular pair of orange hand-me-down pedal pushers that I wore for three summers hating them every time I wore them, and how I resented the time I had to devote to weed pulling, dishwashing, vacuuming, and baby-sitting. I compared myself to Cinderella. There was never enough money for the things that other girls had, the fancy Barbie doll outfits, the Crayola set with 64 crayons, or the mohair sweater that I longed for. Often, I felt different, sad, confused, and angry.

And then there is the delicious part of my childhood that I write about. I am riding my Schwinn downhill, the wind blowing my ponytail straight back, and I am free and on my way to the cold, wide waters of the Wisconsin River for a day of swimming. Or I am walking home beneath the deep, winter skies, toes numbs from another night of ice skating. I can still smell the wet wool of the warming shack and hear the old, corny songs piped from the speakers as we skated dizzy, around and around the rink beneath the dazzling night sky. The snow is piled high around me, and I turn off Foster Street onto Matthew, heading for home and my flannel nightgown and pink fuzzy slippers.

Or it is a quiet summer night, alive with the smells of mowed grass and children's sweat and honeysuckle, and we are playing until our mothers call; red-light-green-light, kick-the-can, ringers, ghost, hide-and-seek. And summer is an endless wash of sunshine and splashing by creeks and rivers or roaming in the woods and chasing fireflies.

Or I remember stopping on the way home from the library, as my sister and I linger at Stanges Park, a magical place. A river wanders through it with dips, and sweet little bridges span the gentle curves, and weeping willows drape the banks. We play house, dipping our dolls clothes in the brown-bottom river. While waiting for tiny diapers and dresses to dry, we eat our humble snack, soda crackers with margarine, and it is delicious beside that gentle, curving river.

And there were ten-cent movies on Saturday afternoon at the Cosmos Theater where we cheered the Three Stooges and the Lone Ranger. And there were Sunday nights of watching *Lassie,* the whistling refrain of the theme song pulling us around the old black-and-white Zenith. Later, we watched *The Ed Sullivan Show* and *Bonanza* and sometimes our dad whipped up a batch of fudge, his specialty.

In *Zen in the Art of Writing*, Ray Bradbury explains that the inspiration for his fiction comes directly from childhood memories. He developed his writing style by stumbling on a method in his early twenties. He began making long lists of memories from his child-hood. These lists of nouns were about terrors and objects and joys that he remembered. The list contained simple nouns like night, crickets, ravine, attic, baby, basement, night train, fog horn, trap door, carnival, dwarf. He would sit with his lists of nouns or memories for a while, then began writing. Eventually a story would emerge from this remembering.

Bradbury writes that he blundered into creativity as blindly as any child learning to walk. His long list of memories and sense impressions gave him a wealth of material to play with. He claims that childhood memories are like dipping into the rain barrel of his past, the more water you dip out, the more flows in. For him, the flow has never ceased.

try this

Write about the rituals and holidays of your childhood. If you get bogged down, keep writing "I remember." Strive for sensory details.

Write about a familiar place from your childhood like your bed-room or your grandmother's kitchen. Again, appeal to all the senses. Often our olfactory sense has a strong, direct connection to memory. What did your childhood smell like?

Welcome Criticism

"I love writing. I never really feel comfortable unless I am either actually writing or have a story going. I could not stop writing."

P.G. WODEHOUSE

Like all writers, I've received my share of rejections, those dreaded messages from an editor. Misery in an envelope. Did it hurt? You bet. And it will hurt the next time. And some days it devastated me and shredded my tender heart. But I got over it. And that's the important point. Rejection is part of the writer's game just like striking out happens every inning in baseball. Rejection is merely someone's opinion of your writing on a certain day. When these nasty missives arrive, we've got to hold tight to this perspective. After all, a rejection is only one person, one moment. That's all. It *could* mean that your writing stinks, or it could be that the editor is having a rotten day, or that he or she can't afford free-lance material.

Writers also need to be selective about their friends and their critique group. Show your work and share your dreams only with people whom you trust. I've learned a few things about whom to spend my time with, and I no longer have room for people who want to make me feel like a loser with their slights and barbs. Or folks who get mean and caustic after the third drink. Or for passive-aggressive types—that strange breed who act as if they care about you while somehow, often charmingly, undermining you. Artists have to be self-protective.

And then there's criticism. Criticism is like taking vitamins, or, more accurately, like drinking castor oil. It tastes lousy, but it does the job. If you're in a worthwhile writing group or class, your fellow writers will criticize your work. They'll complain when you're redundant, vague, unfocused, verbose. They'll hurt your feelings, drive you crazy. It's all part of the game, and you need to learn to accept it. Writers who can't take criticism should find another calling. They're no fun, they make your teeth hurt, they're so offensively annoying. Hanging out with wimpy writers is like enduring an endless wait in a long supermarket line, standing behind an obnoxious kid whose high-pitched demands incite you to near violence.

Get over it. Writing isn't for sissies.

About five years ago I had a student who couldn't handle criticism. If the class and I suggested pointers about her style, she defended herself like a pit bull guarding raw meat. This went on for several weeks, no matter if her work was obtuse or poorly written. You might recognize the type—mostly she wanted to vent about her mother and her pieces reeked with ghostly apparitions descending damp stairways and innocent children gazing into lonely mirrors. She was hostile. She responded to our suggestions by throwing her pen across the room and launching a counter-attack at the class's lack of taste and sensitivity. She sneered at my teaching methods and complained about the examples I used to illustrate my points, including my own work. Since I insist on civility in my classes, that is, nobody can get nasty, she was breaking my rules.

By the fifth week of class, I was dreading this woman's antics, and I had caught a cold and developed an ear infection. At the beginning of the critique session, I pleaded with the class for good behavior, while my head buzzed with fever. Again the student threw a tantrum when her work was criticized. I remember watching her through a haze of misery, my head throbbing, pain blazing inside my ears and wishing the ground would swallow one of us.

The following week a miracle occurred. Usually after the fourth or fifth assignment, most of my students' writing is notably improved. The bad attitude student's writing actually had become better! Finally. Her story was tight, vivid, interesting. All the points we'd discussed in class were illustrated in her new style. She'd wrote in a cleaner, more vivid voice, and I told her so. And she graciously accepted my compliments. I met this woman six months later in another workshop I taught. Her writing was dramatically better, and she acknowledged how my class had focused and improved her writing. And she was finally ready to read her work out loud to other writers. I watched her closely that day and noticed that she laughs more, that she seems to be having fun with her writing.

Sometimes I meet students who are so busy defending their writing and planning counter-attacks at their critics that they miss the helpful information that is offered. Not all criticism is helpful. Not all criticism is just or intelligent. But if you want to become a professional writer you must learn to accept criticism. Graciously. Humbly. Quietly. You don't have to agree with it or rush home and rewrite your piece to please your writers' group or class, but you must acknowledge criticism with grace and courage.

I suggest that anyone who is having his or her work critiqued listen with a closed mouth. Forget defending yourself or telling off your critics. A simple thank you is appropriate. All else is usually a poorly contrived defense. Pay particular attention if your readers keep repeating the same points.

Pay attention to your rejections also. Are the editors saying the same thing as earlier critics of your work? Take a positive tack, learn from rejection. Reconsider the work, rewrite it, read it out loud, then mail it again. Remember, all writers get rejected at some point in their careers. A rejection does not mean you cannot write. A rejection means that somebody isn't buying your work today. Maybe they will tomorrow. Or maybe another editor will buy the same piece. A rejection means that you're trying, that you've got grit, backbone. You put your words on the line, and that's remarkable. A rejection never means give up. It means try again.

try this

Go back and edit some of your earlier work. This exercise works best if you hone works that you wrote at least a few years ago. How has your writing improved? How is your style different now?

Don't Forget Joy

"The anxiety is unbearable. I only hope it lasts forever."

OSCAR WILDE

By now you realize that writing is hard work. All professional writers will tell you the same thing. It's not a glamorous profession. It is often a lonely struggle, a battle with self. Some days I awake and question why I've chosen such a solitary career, sure I can't endure this isolation.

Yet I am rarely more content than when I am writing. The faster I write, the easier the words come, the happier I am. It is exhilarating, it's like flying, making love, eating wonderful food, or holding a baby.

And there is solace and safety in writing. Writing takes place in an inviolable world, a sheltered, warm place that is all our own where we can relax, explore, find ourselves, make friends with our characters, explore issues, know ourselves more deeply.

We can be infinitely kind to ourselves when we write. We can explore all parts of our past and create visions and worlds of unimaginable glory. We can play God. We can commit murder, mayhem, destruction. We can make love to strangers and invent families funnier and more loving than our own. We can play with the unabashed abandonment of a dizzy four year old.

Through writing we can banish our fears, our doubts, the painful years before we found our way with words. We can soothe that former self, the awkward boy who for years was the class nerd. Or set free the ugly duckling twelve year old. Writing erases double chins, buck teeth, flat chests, and wrinkles. We are all beautiful and brave when we write.

There is great joy in writing. All our passions and sorrows and fears have a place, they are transformed into words that grow and grow like sweet ripples in a shallow pond. We are empowered when we recast our troubles or triumphs into words. We are washed clean by this process, stilled and blessed. Yes, blessed. Because writing can be the greatest of

blessings in our lives. In all the serious business of learning how to write and buckling down into a disciplined routine, don't forget the pure delight, the kicks, the thrill, the laughs that come from this work. All in all, it's a damned good time.

And last, remember that writers are part of a long and noble tradition. Our predecessors were scribes, bards, poets, writers. We keep track of things, explain the world to the rest of humanity, open ourselves for the good of all. The world cannot survive and thrive without our brave tribe. It is a worthy calling; there is none better.

try this

Write about who or what you have left behind. Have you grown beyond some of your friendships? Is your lifestyle dramatically different from your parents or siblings?

Last Words

"A mind that is stretched to a new idea never returns to its original dimension."

OLIVER WENDELL HOLMES

By now I hope you realize how important it is to trace your past, discovering in your distant footprints the echoes of the writer you've become. Explore these far-off times and remember the part of you that was most alive and aware. While you're mining your memories, leave your wounds and hurts behind so that your words can turn into wisdom.

Face the fact that there are no gimmicks, gewgaws, or gypsy charms to ease the pain of writing. Writing or any creative endeavor is often painful or at least anxiety-provoking, and the first pages loom as daunting as the first day of a diet or exercise program. But by using a few tricks and techniques, you can sneak past your fears and onto the page. And before you know it, you'll be having so much fun, you'll forget your nervousness and doubts.

If you write professionally, you'll sacrifice and starve along the way, but you need to write anyway. Maybe your bank account will be pitiful, but your soul will be fed, your heart will be light, your mirror will hold the answers. Because a writer will be looking back at you, and that's enough. Because no matter how weird or uncomfortable writing makes you feel, the process and the results are always worth the effort.

By now I hope you understand that you shouldn't sugar coat your family secrets or write for the suits in New York. Write for yourself first, then aim at an audience of people whom you'd like to invite for dinner. Write to make your friends laugh, write so that your children know who you really are, including your "drenching sorrows."

Take your notebook with you wherever you go, noticing, noticing. Banish arrogance from your vocabulary. Learn the basics about sentences and style, language and structure. Write the way you talk, and learn to ruthlessly trim the excess from every sentence. Write for the senses, describing life the way it really is. Describe how it feels when all the snow in the world is falling outside the mountain cabin and how night is a shadow that slows down time and how the smell of wind in your daughter's hair fills you with joy.

Read close and try to understand how other writers think and how their techniques end up on the page. Pay attention to today, not only for your writing but because it too will become part of your memories. Stop making excuses, settle into a sensible routine, and make the necessary sacrifices so that you can write regularly. Add layers to your writing, page after page, day after day. And, no matter what the weather, write out the storm.

Bibliography

Periodicals for Writers:

Poets & Writers, published bi-monthly

Publishers Weekly, published weekly

The Writer, published monthly

Writer's Digest, published monthly

Creativity and Inspiration:

Bradbury, Ray. *Zen in the Art of Writing, Essays on Creativity.* Santa Barbara: Capra Press, 1990.

Brande, Dorthea. *Becoming a Writer.* Los Angeles: Jeremy P. Tarcher, Inc., 1934, reprint 1981.

Cameron, Julia, with Mark Bryan. *The Artist's Way, A Spiritual Path to Higher Creativity.* New York: G.P. Putnam's Sons, 1992.

Cook, Marshall J. *Freeing Your Creativity, A Writer's Guide.* Cincinnati: Writer's Digest Books, 1992.

Dillard, Annie. *The Writing Life.* New York: Harper & Row, 1989.

Edwards, Betty. *Drawing on the Right Side of the Brain.* Los Angeles: Jeremy P. Tarcher, Inc. 1979.

Gawain, Shakti. *Creative Visualization.* Mill Valley: Whatever Publishing, 1986.

Goldberg, Natalie. *Long, Quiet Highway, Waking Up in America.* New York: Bantam Books, 1993.

Goldberg, Natalie. *Wild Mind, Living the Writer's Life.* New York: Bantam Books, 1990.

Goldberg, Natalie. *Writing Down the Bones.* Boston: Shambhala, 1986.

Jeffers, Susan. *Feel the Fear and Do it Anyway.* New York: Fawcett Columbine, 1987.

Lamott, Anne. *Bird by Bird.* New York: Pantheon Books, 1994.

Rico, Gabriele Lusser. *Writing the Natural Way, Using Right-Brain Techniques to Release Your Expressive Powers.* Los Angeles: Jeremy P. Tarcher, Inc., 1983.

Nonfiction and Essay:

Bender, Sheila. *Writing Personal Essays: How to Shape Your Life Experiences for the Page.* Cincinnati: Writer's Digest Books, 1995.

Kelton, Nancy Davidoff. *Writing From Personal Experience, How to Turn Your Life into Salable Prose.* Cincinnati: Writer's Digest Books, 1997.

Zinsser, William. *On Writing Well, An Informal Guide to Writing Nonfiction,* third edition. New York: Harper & Row, 1985.

Tools and Techniques:

Neff, Glenda Tennant, editor. *The Writer's Essential Desk Reference.* Cincinnati: Writer's Digest Books, 1991.

Provost, Gary. *Make Your Words Work.* Cincinnati: Writer's Digest Books, 1990.

Rodale, J.I. *The Synonym Finder.* New York: Warner Books, 1978.

Fiction:

Bernays, Anne, and Pamela Painter. *What If?* New York: Harper Collins, 1995.

Frey, James N. *How to Write a Damn Good Novel.* New York: St. Martin's Press, 1987.

Gardner, John. *The Art of Fiction, Notes on Craft for Young Writers.* New York: Vintage Books, 1985.

Hall, Oakley. *The Art & Craft of Novel Writing.* Cincinnati: Story Press, 1989.

Novaovich, Josip. *The Fiction Writer's Workshop.* Cincinnati: Story Press, 1995.